Contents

Director's Foreword

World-class art, monumental architecture, social history, a domestic atmosphere—the variety that is the Taft Museum is reflected in the essays and illustrations that follow. Whether it is the history of domestic architecture and interior design from the Federal period through the 1920s; the story of a philanthropic couple who devoted their lives to art, music, and public education; the history of art from medieval Europe and the great dynasties of China through painting and sculpture of the early twentieth century—each area provides the reader and museum visitor with an exceptional experience that could not be had elsewhere.

This same variety of experience, which makes the Taft Museum a must for visitors to the city as well as a hometown favorite, brought me to the Taft, first as a member of the Taft Museum Committee and now as director. I am delighted that these volumes will permit even more people to share our love of this unique institution and am grateful to the many people who have made them possible.

The preparation of the manuscript for this catalogue was supported in part by two grants from the National Endowment for the Arts, a federal agency, which were matched by grants from the Corbett Foundation, Cincinnati, and the Getty Grant Program, Santa Monica, California. In addition, the Thomas J. Emery Memorial in Cincinnati provided a generous grant in support of color photography of the permanent collections.

During the ten-year period that the Taft Museum's staff has worked to compile this catalogue of the collections, the museum's administrative staff and advisory committee rose to the challenge of raising the necessary funds to publish these books. The hardbound edition has been made possible with generous grants from local philanthropic and corporate foundations, including the Louise Taft Semple Foundation; the Eleanora C.U. Alms Trust, Fifth Third Bank, Trustee; the Greater Cincinnati Foundation; the Robert and Adele Schiff Foundation; and the Ohio Valley Foundation. In addition, the Getty Grant Program, which had previously funded the preparation of the manuscript, continued to support this project by providing a second grant to help offset publication costs.

Members of the extended Taft family were instrumental in securing grants and contributed personally to this project. The management of the Taft Museum and the Cincinnati Institute of Fine Arts acknowledges the generous gifts made by Mr. and Mrs. John T. Lawrence, Jr., Mr. and Mrs. John T. Lawrence III, Mrs. Margo Tytus, Mr. and Mrs. Robert A. Taft II, and Mr. Seth C. Taft.

Two longtime members of the Taft Museum Committee and devoted patrons of the Taft Museum provided much needed advice and funding for this project: Dr. Martin and Dr. Carol M. Macht and Mr. and Mrs. John W. Warrington.

A separate fund-raising campaign was initiated to produce an economically accessible softcover edition of this research for the Cincinnati public. The paperbound edition of this catalogue was made possible with grants from the Procter & Gamble Fund and the National Endowment for the Humanities, a federal agency. We are grateful to both of these supporters for understanding and endorsing our desire to have these books readily available to our local audiences.

Phillip C. Long, DIRECTOR

Preface

For sixty years the Taft Museum has welcomed its visitors to the display of an international collection of fine arts objects housed in a landmark building. The people of Cincinnati, to whom by its charter the museum was given, as well as regional visitors and travelers from all over the world, have found here the personal collection of a local couple, Anna Sinton and Charles Phelps Taft, whose dedication to public enjoyment of the arts was manifested not only through the museum that bears their name but also through their many other philanthropies.

As the museum approached its sixtieth anniversary, the museum administration recognized the need for a comprehensive publication that would document not only the artistic treasures of the collection but also the motivations of our founders in creating an art museum. We felt that two perspectives on that activity would be required. To that end, we have endeavored to write a history of our museum that both the general audience and the scholar can use. We know that this publication, like all our public programs, must reach out to those in our potential audience who have either not yet visited us or not known of the museum's existence.

This catalogue supersedes a handbook published in the early years of our public history and subsequently reissued with slight revisions. Our goal has been to make a record of new expert opinions, informed by international research standards and presented in a style that our public can enjoy. From the outset we have planned to publish the catalogue in both hard- and paperbound editions. The latter edition is available in four separate volumes that give readers the opportunity to purchase them as their interests dictate. The first volume of this series tells the story of the successive residents of the Baum-Taft House and how it became a museum open to many visitors, even in the Tafts' lifetimes. This volume is followed by three more that focus on the separate fields of the collection—the paintings, the decorative arts, and the Chinese ceramics. Each is introduced by an essay that explains why the Tafts selected these rare and beautiful objects to decorate their home and enrich their lives.

To assist us in telling the story of the Taft Museum, we have selected a team of specialists who could verify the excellent quality of the majority of our holdings. Being truthful, they had also to tell us that certain paintings, porcelains, and pieces of jewelry, for example, must now be acknowledged as deliberate fakes, while others are genuine but only the product of a workshop and not from a master's hand. Glancing over the catalogue entries on every object we learn that the Tafts were, on the whole, fortunate in their purchases and that their mistakes were no greater or more frequent than the errors of judgment made by other collectors of their time (and since). The usefulness of such entries to the contemporary reader is that they may stimulate more careful investigation in personal collecting, while they should encourage the taking of an occasional risk on an unsigned but perfectly convincing work of art.

Furthermore, we asked our catalogue authors to explain to current audiences the significance of our collection within the context of the art-collecting practices of Americans in the first quarter of this century. The Tafts were by no means the only wealthy couple who could buy valuable things and endow public museums through their generosity, nor were they the richest. But occasionally they did make a purchase that earned them the envy of other great collectors.

In preparing this publication, we have also considered the growing public interest in historic preservation of both architecture and interior design. Thus, to the list of specialists in the fields of European old-master paintings, decorative arts, and Chinese ceramics we have added contributions from those who have studied the history of American architecture, furniture, and domestic decoration. The Taft Museum is rare for its combination of features: early-nineteenth-century American domestic architecture; examples of European and American interior furnishings and decoration, including unique mural paintings from the mid-nineteenth century; and the display of a world-famous collection of art works dating from about 1250 to 1906. The thoughtful integration of this ensemble has earned the Taft Museum its international reputation.

The research phase of the preparation of this publication has already prompted us to make many changes in the presentation and interpretation of our collections and our house to attract the new audiences that await us. Reevaluation of two fields, the Chinese porcelains and the European ornamented wares and watches, has led to displays that focus the viewer's attention more on aspects of their manufacture and decoration than was previously the case. The paintings will be reordered in the galleries to highlight some often overlooked masterpieces and to create chronological and stylistic groupings. And gallery renovations already underway are designed to enhance the federal-period atmosphere of the Baum-Taft house.

This publication is therefore more than an accumulation of scholarly detail—the factual matters of attribution and authenticity—although it certainly affirms the regard our professional colleagues have long shown our collections. The Taft Museum has always embodied the wisdom, vision, and capacity for enjoyment of the arts that our founders possessed. Their love of the arts and their further commitment to sharing the collection with the public has become the modern Taft Museum's mission, exemplified by these volumes. More than just a set of books, this catalogue offers us the opportunity to renew our faithfulness to Charles and Anna Taft's commitment to art and its role in public education.

Ruth Krueger Meyer, DIRECTOR

Acknowledgments

Over the course of more than a decade, many friends and colleagues have given unstintingly of their advice and encouragement toward the making of this publication. As in any attempt to express thanks for a project of this magnitude, some names will inadvertently be omitted, but it is hoped that everyone who participated in even the smallest way will feel recompensed by seeing the work accomplished.

For myself, the organization of the publication was done in payment of the debt one owes one's mentor for the inspiration that shapes and guides one's career. Professor Fred Licht, Boston University, was among the first to hear of my appointment as director of the Taft Museum in 1983. During our subsequent phone conversation, we discussed the need for a new catalogue of the museum's collections, and he signed on as editor. Although Licht was later forced to withdraw from his editorial role, his appointed successor, Dr. Edward J. Sullivan, professor of art history at New York University, carried through with dedication and enthusiasm.

Of singular importance to the success of our publication has been the participation of Paul Anbinder, president of Hudson Hills Press, New York. As our publisher, Anbinder endorsed our decision to set the highest standards for the project, and he steadfastly retained and reinforced that commitment. He brought to the publication the sensitive editorial skills of Fronia W. Simpson, whose challenges to our scholars burnished their entries and resolved many issues of documentation.

Through the participation of our team of scholars, the significance of this publication for the museum was greatly magnified. Their visits to Cincinnati for research and public lectures afforded our staff opportunities to examine objects in the collection with them, hear their musings, and thereby profit from their experience. Many of them have since provided consultation on a variety of topics ranging from conservation to exhibitions and interpretation. Collectively, they have helped to reshape our education program and gallery installations.

Several museum colleagues and independent scholars deserve special recognition for their assistance in identifying writers for the European decorative arts. Olga Raggio, chair of the department of European sculpture and decorative arts at the Metropolitan Museum of Art, New York, sagely guided our selection of members of her department to write various entries in this difficult area of connoisseurship. Winthrop Kelly Edy, New York, identified his colleague Jonathan Snellenburg as the appropriate expert for the Taft Museum's collection of watches.

Special praise and gratitude must be expressed for the efforts of the Taft Museum staff and members of the Taft Museum Committee who have been involved in this catalogue. Assistant Director/Curator of Collections David Torbet Johnson seconded the project in every conceivable way, from fund-raising through endless research in support of scholars. He took up recalcitrant objects that would not disclose the secrets of their manufacture and matured his own scholarship in the process. With the death of Anthony Derham, Johnson, working in collaboration with Anthony du Boulay, completed the section of this catalogue devoted to Chinese ceramics and works of art. These tasks were done while Johnson simultaneously served as registrar and participated in every facet of curatorial and administrative work at the museum.

Catherine L. O'Hara joined the museum staff primarily to copyedit the scholars' manuscripts. She has remained as publications editor and press officer and has written essays for other museum publications. O'Hara has been relentless in her determination to deliver a perfect manuscript, and the reader will greatly benefit from her sensitivity and attention to detail. Abby S. Schwartz assisted with the laborious process of searching for and identifying all the photographic illustrations and preparing their captions while meeting her responsibilities as curator of education. Tony Walsh joined the museum's staff as photographer during the preparation of this catalogue. He has photographed with a sensitive eye nearly every object in the collection as well as most installations. Anthony Lauro, Columbus, Ohio, also provided photographs for this catalogue, including the Duncanson murals.

Among the members of the Taft Museum Committee who showed constant concern for the welfare of the catalogue, I must thank Dr. Carol M. Macht, curator emerita of the Cincinnati Art Museum; Anne Lawrence, great-granddaughter of the museum's founders; Phillip C. Long, my successor as director of the Taft Museum; Robert Stautberg, chairman of the committee; and Sallie Wadsworth, secretary/treasurer.

Because this publication is divided into four sections representing the history of the museum and its collections, special recognition must be given to outside readers and other consultants for each field. Section one, *The History of the Collections and the Baum-Taft House,* benefited from consultation with Heather Hallenberg, former curator of education at the Taft Museum; William Seale, Washington, D.C.; Elizabeth Tuttle and Walter Langsam, Cincinnati; Dr. Zane Miller, professor of history at the University of Cincinnati; Kenneth Trapp, curator of crafts and decorative arts, The Oakland Museum, California; Jayne Merkel, New York; and Colin Streeter, New York.

Section two, *European and American Paintings:* Dr. John H. Wilson, curator of paintings and sculpture, Cincinnati Art Museum; Dr. Gabriel Weisberg, department of art history, University of Minnesota, Minneapolis; Dr. Robert L. Herbert, department of art history, Yale University, New Haven, Connecticut; Madeleine Fidell-Beaufort and Robert Hellebranth, Paris; and Dr. Martha Wolff, curator of European painting before 1750, The Art Institute of Chicago.

Section three, *European Decorative Arts:* Yvonne Hackenbroch, London; Dr. James Draper and Clare Le Corbeiller, curators of European sculpture and decorative arts, The Metropolitan Museum of Art; Hugh Tait, keeper, Waddesdon Bequest, British Museum, London; Anna Somers Cocks, editor-in-chief, *Art Papers,* London; Charles Truman, Christie's, London; Madeleine Marcheix, director emerita, Musée Municipal de l'Evêché, Limoges; Véronique Notin, director, Musée Municipal de l'Evêché; Doreen Stoneham, Research Laboratory for Archaeology and the History of Art, Oxford, England; and Otto C. Thieme, curator of costume and textiles, Cincinnati Art Museum.

Section four, *Chinese Ceramics and Works of Art:* Sheila Keppel, Oakland; Dr. Stephen Little, curator, Asian art, Honolulu Academy of Arts; Dr. Julia B. Curtis, Williamsburg, Virginia; Terese Tse Bartholomew, curator of Indian art, Asian Art Museum of San Francisco; Suzanne Valenstein, research curator of Asian art, The Metropolitan Museum of Art; and Ellen Avril, associate curator of Far Eastern art, Cincinnati Art Museum.

Ruth Krueger Meyer

Editor's Introduction

At a time when art exhibitions have taken the form of media events, and great attention is paid to the enormous prices paid for pictures, some scholars and the public often seem to neglect the permanent collections of museums. Among the basic tasks of the art historian are the study, interpretation, and categorization of works of art so that others can carry out further analytical research. Catalogues of the permanent collections of museums are indispensable for both experts and members of the interested general public. For historians to do their work, they must know not only the location of works of art but also such empirical facts as to their size, media, date, and provenance. The bringing together of such material and extending its significance with historical interpretation should result in a catalogue that serves as a point of departure for a broader historical network of ideas.

Now, when the emphasis of art-historical publication appears to be weighted toward the explication of theoretical aspects of art, the essential labor of cataloguing is not given the credit it deserves. The rewards of such projects, however, are obvious. This catalogue of the Taft Museum is the result of over six years of intensive work on the part of thirty authors and additional experts who have served as consultants. Virtually every aspect of the museum is covered in its pages, from the history of the house and the acquisition habits of the Taft family to an examination of the myriad paintings, sculptures, and decorative-arts objects in the collections.

The Taft Museum, one of the outstanding small museums in the United States, possesses a collection that, in many areas, rivals those of the great artistic institutions both in this country and abroad. As with all significant personal collections such as those of Henry Clay Frick, Isabella Stewart Gardner, or Archer Milton Huntington, specific patterns of acquisition have lent a definite personality to the Taft collection. The Tafts, for instance, had a special fondness for Dutch and Flemish old-master paintings, nineteenth-century French landscapes, and Chinese porcelains. Their affection does not mean they neglected other areas. A strength of the Taft Museum is its eclecticism (typical of collections formed by nineteenth- and early-twentieth-century buyers of art), which provides the visitor (and the reader of these volumes) with a wealth of visual material concerning many periods of time, numerous nations, and a wide variety of manifestations of artistic sensibility.

In its earlier years, the Taft Museum benefited from the care and intelligence of Walter Siple, who served as the institution's first director. Under his aegis, an initial catalogue was published in 1939. In 1958 it was updated with information on provenance and exhibitions provided by Katherine Hanna, the museum's second director. This handbook provided a useful guide for visitors to the Taft for many years. In 1983 Ruth Krueger Meyer, the third director, envisioned an ambitious cataloguing project with full scholarly apparatus for every object in the museum. I was honored to be invited to be the editor of this catalogue and have learned a great deal about the collection in the process. But, more importantly, working with the material and consulting with the authors have expanded my understanding of many facets of the history of art. The all-embracing scope of the catalogue will certainly have a similar effect on its readers. We hope that the catalogue, through its wide-ranging discussions of numerous artistic phenomena, will not only serve to deepen the public's knowledge of what is contained within the walls of the Taft Museum but also stimulate thought and curiosity about the very nature of artistic expression.

Edward J. Sullivan
New York University

THE TAFT MUSEUM

CHINESE CERAMICS AND WORKS OF ART

The Taft Collection of Chinese Porcelains

Anthony du Boulay

It is uncertain when the first Chinese ceramics reached the West, but trade between the Han and Roman empires existed over the Silk Route two thousand years ago. The earliest-known porcelains still existing in Europe are contemporary with Marco Polo, the Venetian explorer of the late thirteenth century, but it was not until the sixteenth century and the arrival in China of the Portuguese that quantities of Chinese blue-and-white porcelain started to arrive in the West. The trade greatly increased during the seventeenth century when the Dutch East India Company became the chief merchants in the Far East. However, the fall of the Ming dynasty in 1644 and the ensuing civil war in South China meant that very little porcelain was made during the third quarter of the century, and the Dutch turned to Japan for their porcelain.

In 1675 Jingdezhen, the center of the Chinese porcelain industry, was substantially destroyed during the Wu Sanguei rebellion. Therefore, in 1680 the young Kangxi emperor set up a commission to study the porcelain industry, and in 1682 he appointed Cang Yingxuan superintendent of the kilns to modernize and revitalize the industry. His original responsibility was to make the factories efficient rather than to change the artistic nature of the porcelain, although this development came later. Within a very short time, China regained the major share of the porcelain trade with the West by undercutting the Japanese prices and by producing a thinner, whiter, and altogether superior porcelain. The Japanese share of the market started to decline in about 1690 and had virtually disappeared by 1740.

At first the Chinese adapted domestic models for export to Europe but gradually were persuaded by the Dutch East India Company merchants to produce both shapes and decoration especially for the West. Therefore, by about 1730 at the latest, the blue-and-white porcelain had ceased to be made, with the exception of the cheap and coarser dinnerwares, and famille verte, made between 1680 and 1730, had been superseded by famille rose.

In earlier times ceramics were produced at numerous sites in both north and south China. However, beginning in the thirteenth century, Jingdezhen became the chief porcelain manufactory, although pottery was still made elsewhere. Situated toward the south of China, about equidistant between Beijing (then Peking) and Canton, Jingdezhen by the middle of the eighteenth century was a city with over a million inhabitants, but only a single industry, porcelain manufacturing. With the advent of the Industrial Revolution in England and the introduction of Josiah Wedgwood's creamware, trade with Europe greatly declined at the end of the eighteenth century, being sustained only by the North American market.

Père d'Entrecolles, one of the Jesuit priests in China, writing in 1712 and again in 1722 during the latter part of the reign of Kangxi, gives a fascinating and vivid picture of the process, describing the kilns and the composition of the porcelain, the crushing of the rock, and the mining of kaolin. He explains how the porcelain was mass-produced and decorated and how a single piece might pass through the hands of seventy workers before completion. He also gives a description of the various molds and how the decorators were graded according to their skills.[1] Designs were taken from many sources, including nature, but elaborate scenes were done by copying wood-block prints from stories popular in China at the time. Today in Jingdezhen, at least one modern china factory still uses eighteenth-century methods of production, decoration, and types of kilns, although there are primarily modern electric-fired kilns producing everyday china.

European interest in porcelain increased tremendously in the second half of the seventeenth century, and each ruler wished to install in the royal palace a porcelain room crammed with every manner of Asian ceramics; those at Potsdam and Pommersfelden are still in existence. Queen Mary of England was in the forefront of this fashion and installed such a room at Hampton Court, but after her premature death in 1694 the collection was dispersed. By the middle of the nineteenth century this taste had fallen into such disfavor that Lord Macaulay, writing about the queen, said that she "amused herself by forming at Hampton Court a vast collection of hideous images, and of vases on which houses, trees, bridges and mandarins were depicted in outrageous defiance of all laws of perspective."[2] However, within a quarter of a century of the publication of his book, these "hideous images" and "outrageous" vases had started to come back into fashion to such an extent that they were being bought up all over Europe, as well as from temples and private collections throughout China, which had been and was to be ravaged by both civil and colonialist wars for a hundred years from the late 1830s onward.

Although some imperial porcelains reached the West after the sacking of the Summer Palace in 1860, it was only after the Boxer Rebellion of 1900 that Westerners started to see the finest of the Ming and Qing wares. In fact, it took the great exhibition of Chinese art at Burlington House, London, in 1935 to open the eyes of Europeans fully to the difference between the imperial and the domestic and export wares. At the same time, it was only with the building of the railway network across China in the early years of the present century that the richness of China's more remote past was discovered. Although many of the most spectacular tombs and artifacts have been discovered only since 1949 and are retained in China, some American museums were fortunate to have had gifted directors and curators who acquired many of the greatest treasures of this type.

The Tafts had finished collecting by the time most of these fine Ming and Qing wares started to appear on the market, and with very few exceptions, such as the two Tang ladies (1931.143, 145, p. 574) and the peach blooms and other monochromes, they never entered into either of these fields. Nevertheless, within the scope of domestic and export porcelains, they were able to gather some remarkable pieces.

The approximately two hundred examples of Chinese porcelain in the Taft Museum are typical of a rich man's collection formed at the beginning of the twentieth century. By far the majority of pieces date from or were attributed at the time of purchase to the period of the Kangxi emperor (1662–1722). Nearly half are decorated with the colors known as famille verte, famille jaune, and famille noire. The fashion for this kind of porcelain began during the last twenty years of the nineteenth century, and competition between James A. Garland in America and George Salting in England, together with their respective dealers, caused an enormous jump in price. The Garland collection was acquired largely through Henry Duveen, who set up shop first in Boston in 1876 and then in New York in 1879, while Murray Marks in London bought for Salting. Edgar Gorer then began dealing, and his competition with Duveen helped raise the market for Kangxi porcelain, particularly famille noire, to a theretofore unknown level. Related porcelains also rose considerably in price, but most types of Chinese porcelain and pottery that are admired now remained comparatively unknown and unappreciated then.

Through Duveen, the Garland collection, after his death, was mainly acquired by J. Pierpont Morgan. At Pierpont Morgan's death, his collection was bought in 1914–15, again through Duveen, by three rich Americans — John D. Rockefeller, Henry Clay Frick, and P. A. B. Widener — who were reported to have paid $3,350,000 for it. However, parts of the collection must have been sold off, since certain of the Morgan pieces were acquired by the Tafts in 1915, while other pieces went elsewhere. Another great collector of that period was Benjamin Altman, many of whose finest pieces are now in the Metropolitan Museum of Art, New York. The Salting collection had gone at a slightly earlier date to the Victoria and Albert Museum, London, although the Taft has two pieces originally from his collection. In England, James Orrock, a watercolor artist, as well as his much more famous contemporary James McNeill Whistler, also collected porcelains. One of Whistler's patrons, Louis Huth, had a fine collection, which was sold at auction in 1905.

Anna Sinton and Charles Phelps Taft acquired nearly one-third of their collection from Duveen during 1902. The rest was bought at irregular intervals, with the last acquisition arriving just over a quarter of a century later in 1928, just after the time of the Tafts' deed of gift of their collections, house, and the land on which it stands to the citizens of Cincinnati.

To the student of the history of art acquisition, the Taft Museum collections of Chinese porcelains, European and American paintings, and European decorative arts are particularly important. Being virtually unchanged and unaltered in content and method of display, they show the ideals and breadth of collecting of well-traveled Americans during the first twenty-five years of the twentieth century. The other notable collection in which porcelain is shown along with furniture and pictures is the Frick Collection in New York. Frick, however, was obviously far less interested in Chinese porcelain than the Tafts, and his examples are therefore rather weak in comparison with his superb old-master paintings and French furniture. In many other cases, such as the Salting collection in the Victoria and Albert Museum, the porcelain is displayed together in a gallery rather than interspersed with pictures, furniture, and other artworks, while the Altman collection in the Metropolitan Museum is shown as only part of the larger Chinese collection. A more apt comparison might be the collection at the Lady Lever Art Gallery, Port Sunlight Village (Wirral, Merseyside, England).

During the early twentieth century, the study of Chinese art was still in a nascent stage, and thus collectors, dealers, and museum officials were hampered by a lack of information. As a result, virtually all collections of this date have a fair sprinkling of pieces that we now consider to be either of a later period or deliberate fakes and forgeries. Other pieces that were then considered to be rare and unusual are now known to be fairly commonplace and have become unfashionable.

The Taft collection, however, contains some real masterpieces of potting and decoration. Among the glazed famille verte vessels, the exceptionally tall rouleau vase (1931.160, p. 644), brilliantly enameled with a battle scene from the story of Wang Meng, a hero of the Han dynasty, is particularly important. A smaller rouleau vase (1931.162, p. 637) has delightful scenes taken directly from wood-block prints depicting rice cultivation and silkworm feeding. One lantern (1931.86, pp. 633–34), beautifully painted with an audience scene, exemplifies the extraordinarily delicate porcelain that artisans were able to make at the end of Kangxi's reign. The pair of triple-gourd vases (1931.34, 38, p. 652) shows the more restrained type of famille verte decoration in which flowers are simply and gracefully reserved on a green ground. Among a series of pieces with powder blue, or *bleu soufflé*, grounds, a pair of rouleau vases painted with ladies on terraces is particularly attractive (1931.169, 173, p. 655). The way in which the ladies, with their fine black hair piled on top of their heads, are painted is exemplary of the finest Kangxi famille verte decoration.

The magnificent garniture of three baluster vases with covers and two beakers with famille noire grounds (1931.148–52, pp. 670–71) shows how beautiful this family of colors can be when genuine (although one cover is a nineteenth-century Samson copy and the other two appear to have been married to their vases). It is believed that only two other comparable garnitures exist, one now in the Dallas Museum of Art and one formerly in the Morgan and Rockefeller collections.[3] These vases are particularly useful in identifying genuine famille noire, since the famille verte reserved panels enameled over the glaze are unquestionably of the period. Of all the Chinese porcelains, famille noire is the most difficult to authenticate. The enormous prices paid for it at the beginning of this century meant that it was faked and imitated — sometimes very skillfully — more than any other kind of porcelain. The opaque enamels easily covered previous decoration, and the best copies are genuine vases from which the original, less popular decoration was stripped off with acid so that the new famille noire design could be added. Some scholars have suggested that not one of the famille noire vases in the Frick Collection is genuine, and certainly a number from the Salting collection are no longer considered to be of the period.

Since the Taft collection contains many pieces of famille noire as well as similar pieces with yellow and green grounds enameled directly on the biscuit, it is useful for teaching connoisseurship. The two wine ewers or teapots (1931.1, 1931.5, p. 665) as well as two beakers (1931.2, 4, p. 664) are of a type identified in early European inventories and therefore accepted by all knowledgeable scholars of Chinese porcelain as being of the period. One can also be fairly positive about a large baluster vase (1931.147, p. 668), which, although heavily damaged, is like one in the Franks collection in the British Museum that was acquired before most scholars believe that copies first began to be made.

The Taft collection also has a very fine group of famille verte figures enameled on the biscuit, among them a pair of boys standing holding later lotus-flower nozzles (1931.6, 10, p. 624). These are of a type supposedly showing Westerners and possibly do represent people from the Indian subcontinent. A fine, large pair of Buddhistic lions (1948.1–2, p. 623) and, among the figures of Immortals, a particularly attractive example of Guanyin sitting on a hexagonal pedestal (1931.44, pp. 616–17) and one of the god of war, Guandi (1931.33, p. 615), exhibit the dexterity of the Chinese artisan in modeling and the skill of the painter in decoration. Particularly amusing is a figure that has lost its original head, which has been replaced by one of blanc de chine (1931.24, p. 620). The blanc de chine, in fact, would have been made at Dehua in the south of China, some three or four hundred miles from Jingdezhen where the rest of the figure was made, although they are probably both contemporary, dating from the first few years of the eighteenth century. The technique of combining various genuine fragments to make a whole was used by Lazare Duvaux in Paris during the mid-eighteenth century, when he mounted old pieces of porcelain in ormolu, sometimes combining examples from China, Japan, and Germany with French flowers. In the case of the Taft figure, this marriage was probably made at the end of the nineteenth century.

A fascinating pair of vases (1931.140, 146, pp. 642–43) nearly thirty inches high is decorated in famille verte and modeled in relief with battle scenes. Although exhibited as nineteenth-century pieces for many years, they are probably genuine of the late Kangxi period. The enamels and the manner in which they are made are typical of the early years of the eighteenth century, although the slightly dimpled surface of the porcelain is normally associated with the late eighteenth or early nineteenth century. Documented precedents would nevertheless support an earlier dating.

The blue-and-white porcelain in the Taft collection is almost entirely of the Kangxi period, although two small reticulated wine cups with biscuit figures in relief date from the late Ming dynasty, at the beginning of the seventeenth century (1931.66, 1931.70, p. 578). Two oviform jars with covers, reserved with prunus branches on a pulsating sapphire blue ground (1931.11, 1931.15, pp. 578, 579), are a type that was much admired during the first quarter of the twentieth century. Because they were so popular at that date, they were frequently copied and soon fell out of favor. The jars in the Taft Museum, however, are striking for the beauty of the blue ground. Today, it is quite easy to tell the difference between genuine examples of these jars and the copies, because the color and the glaze were too difficult to reproduce accurately. As a result, although the type is well represented in the major museums, jars of this quality are very rare in private collections. The most striking piece of blue-and-white porcelain in the Taft Museum is a very large *yanyan* vase painted with ladies riding; scholar-officials watch from behind a trellis screen (1931.138, pp. 586–87). Not only are the color and proportions superb, but the vase is beautifully and interestingly painted with a scene taken from a Song dynasty painting: when the Yang family males were unable to go into battle, the women trained to take their places. There is also a garniture of three slender baluster vases with covers (1931.187, 191, p. 584, and 1931.189, p. 585) and two beakers (1931.188, 190, p. 583) painted with the *Lange Lijsen* (long stupids or Long Elizas), which have been popular among Dutch collectors from the beginning of the eighteenth century to the present day.

The collection of porcelain from the later eighteenth century, while not extensive, is represented by a few outstanding pieces. The Yongzheng period is particularly well exemplified by a small series of eggshell plates and saucer dishes painted in Canton with figures (1931.97, p. 676, and 1931.114, 116, pp. 676–77) and quail (1931.95, 99, pp. 676–77) in landscapes. These dishes, which were exported to Europe during the second quarter of the eighteenth century, became very fashionable during the later part of the nineteenth; and when perfect (their extreme thinness renders them very fragile) they are still highly admired by connoisseurs of Chinese porcelain. A magnificent pair of chargers (1931.184–85, p. 675) dating from the late 1720s has scenes from *The Romance of the Western Chamber* finely painted in the centers. In the mainstream of early-twentieth-century taste, a pair (1931.178, 182, p. 679) and two single baluster vases (1931.180, 183, pp. 679, 678) are of a type imported during the eighteenth century in sets of five. These examples are painted with panels of cockerels, flowers, and figures reserved on soufflé ruby grounds. Originally thought to have come from the Forbidden City and to have been made during the reign of Emperor Qianlong, two large jars (1931.166–67, pp. 682–83) with millefleurs, or one thousand flowers, decoration are more typical of the painting done during the reign of his successor, Jiaqing. Despite this slightly later date, they are nevertheless magnificent examples of the heavily decorated Manchu taste of the middle of the Qing period.

The Taft collection contains several figures of birds, including an example of a Kangxi gaming cock poised ready for a fight (1931.45, p. 622). The brightly colored pheasant (1931.181, pp. 680–81) and hawk (1931.179, p. 680), which date to the middle of Emperor Qianlong's reign, show the fine models that were popular in the great houses of Europe during the second half of the eighteenth century.

The Taft peach-bloom collection is one of the finest in the world, although not as extensive as that in the Metropolitan Museum of Art. These, like the famille noire, have been subject to great debate. After close examination, today's scholars would probably not accept every piece in this collection as being authentic, but the quality of the peach-bloom color on all the pieces is particularly fine. The Taft possesses seven of the eight prescribed shapes of objects for a scholar's writing table. The eighth shape itself is the subject of discussion but is probably that of a vase in the Altman bequest to the Metropolitan Museum (inv. no. 14.40.362) with a dragon around its neck. One of the shapes, the water coupe with a recessed neck, is found in the Taft collection in clair de lune (1931.120, p. 611) rather than peach bloom. A small selection of other monochromes of good quality includes a bottle covered in the true *langyao* glaze (1931.107, pp. 602–3), which is much better than the average oxblood color. Today, the fashion in monochromes is for those made for the emperor himself, which, although available at a price to the modern collector, were much more difficult to find while the Tafts were collecting. They were nonetheless able to obtain a lovely Qianlong beaker of archaic *gu* form covered in a magnificent kingfisher blue glaze (1931.115, pp. 607–8). A pair of bottles with an almost white clair-de-lune glaze is imperial and also has the mark of Qianlong's predecessor, Yongzheng (1931.119, 121, p. 612).

The early potteries of the Tang dynasty had only just started appearing on the market when the Tafts were collecting. Therefore, they only purchased one pair of figures of ladies from this period (1931.143, 1931.145, p. 574), although this type of Tang pottery is well represented in other American museums. During the early twentieth century, a type of porcelaneous stoneware with medium-temperature glazes applied on the biscuit, called *fahua,* with little walls of clay, or *cloisons,* was very popular. In the early literature, all these wares are dated to the fifteenth or early sixteenth century. As the sixteenth century continued, many of these pieces were made of a coarser ware, and the three examples in the Taft collection, formerly dated to about 1500, are more probably late sixteenth or early seventeenth century in date. One of the most famous of these pieces, a pear-shaped vase with dragon handles and flowers in relief on the lower part (1931.21, p. 577), is illustrated by R. L. Hobson in his book on Ming porcelain.[4]

One piece of Chinese porcelain in the Taft collection has great historical importance. A ewer in the form of a phoenix is one of the earliest figural pieces to be recorded in European inventories (1931.18, p. 575). This ewer is virtually identical to one that appears in the Saxon royal inventory from before 1640, and it is possibly a piece mentioned in the late sixteenth century. The Taft phoenix has a silver-gilt cover and mounts, which date to the seventeenth century with later additions.

The Taft collection was formed by modern standards along prescribed lines. Fewer than five percent of the pieces date from before the Qing dynasty, and over half are from a single reign, that of the Kangxi emperor. Although many of the pieces were probably exported at the time of manufacture, the collection does not include any examples of armorial porcelain, or what used to be known as Oriental Lowestoft. Nor, with the exception of some of the monochromes, does it include pieces made for the emperor or for the court. A great number of the wares and figures of Immortals were made for use in temples or by the middle class in China at the time. It is known from records that many pieces of this type were exported to Europe, particularly during the reign of Kangxi, before European merchants were able to specify exactly what they needed. For a collection established within this narrow definition, the Taft Museum has many beautiful and important examples.

Notes

See Glossary, pp. 692–96, for definitions of specific terms found in both this essay and the following entries.

1. Many translations of Père d'Entrecolles's writings exist. The easiest to find is Stephen W. Bushell, M.D., *Oriental Ceramic Art: Collection of W. T. Walters*, 1st ed., New York, 1899, New York, 1980, pp. 332–58.

2. Thomas Babington Macaulay, *History of England from the Accession of James II*, 5 vols., London, 1849–61, chap. XI, quoted in Arthur Lane, "Queen Mary's Porcelain Collection at Hampton Court," *Transactions of the Oriental Ceramic Society*, vol. XXV (1949–50), pp. 21–22.

3. Sold from a New York private collection, Sotheby's New York, Nov. 27, 1990, no. 187, for $71,500.

4. R. L. Hobson, *The Wares of the Ming Dynasty*, New York, 1923, pl. 52, fig. 1.

Chinese Ceramics

Descriptions: Anthony Derham
Commentary: David Torbet Johnson

Tang, Liao, and Ming Dynasty Polychromes

Female Attendants

Tang dynasty (618–906), 675–750
Pottery, H. (each) 24.6 cm (9¾ in.)
Unmarked

Each figure of this pair of molded and glazed buff pottery female attendants is standing with her hands together under a long scarf that falls below her knees.

Members of the wealthy, sophisticated Tang dynasty society sought to surround themselves even in death with the splendid riches that they had enjoyed during life. Preparations for the tomb, which usually began well in advance of death, included the purchase of numerous pottery *mingqi,* or "articles of the spirit,"[1] such as replicas of servants and musicians, models of domestic and foreign animals, guardian spirits, vessels, and objects from everyday life. These *Female Attendants* represent retainers who would have continued to serve the deceased in the afterlife.

Made from pressing soft clay into simple bivalve molds and then luting the two sections together along the side seams, these *sancai,* or three-color, figures are covered with polychrome lead glazes over white slip. Characteristic of Tang pottery from this period are the minutely crackled glazes. The unglazed heads, with traces of pigment in the ribboned butterfly chignons, were molded separately and then fitted into the cavities between the shoulders. Originally the faces of these female attendants would have been more extensively painted to create a sense of individuality, but the pigment has since worn off.

1. Candace J. Lewis, *Into the Afterlife: Han and Six Dynasties Chinese Tomb Sculpture from the Schloss Collection,* exh. cat., Vassar College Art Gallery, Poughkeepsie, N.Y., 1990, p. 18.

Provenance [Parish-Watson, New York]; Taft collection, Nov. 9, 1923.
Literature *Catalogue of the Taft Museum,* Cincinnati, 1939 and 1958, nos. 294, 296.

1931.143, 1931.145

1931.143, 145

Bottle Vase

Liao dynasty (907–1125), 1060–1125
Pottery, H. 16.5 cm (6½ in.)
Unmarked

The body of this pear-shaped bottle vase is incised and glazed in green and amber on cream, green, and amber grounds with bold flowering branch sprays. The buff-colored terra-cotta body is dressed in white slip where it is unglazed at the base and flaring foot. The slender trumpet neck, originally attached to the body with lute, is now missing.

The Chinese dynastic name of Liao was adopted in 947 by the unified Khitan tribes inhabiting Manchuria, as their military forces enlarged landholdings to include portions of northern China. The decoration of the Taft vase illustrates contact between the Liao culture and the late Tang dynasty in the uses of polychrome lead glazes over white slip. Characteristic of Liao wares dating after about 1060 are the clearly incised outlines and carefully applied colored glazes of the flower-spray decoration.[1]

1. Margaret Medley, *T'ang Pottery and Porcelain,* London, 1981, p. 136.

Provenance [Parish-Watson, New York]; Taft collection, Nov. 9, 1923.

1931.144

Literature *Catalogue of the Taft Museum,* Cincinnati, 1939 and 1958, no. 295.

1931.144

1931.18

Phoenix Ewer

Ming dynasty (1368–1644), 1570–80
Porcelain with silver-gilt mounts (Nuremberg, ca. 1600, with later additions), H. 29.8 cm (11¾ in.)
Unmarked; mounts marked fh in rectangle and eight-pointed star punch

This ewer is molded as the mythical phoenix, an emblem of the empress, perched among clouds billowing around a rockwork base. More clouds form the neck of the ewer, another long wisp makes the loop handle, and the bird's head is the spout. It is enameled in pale green, turquoise, yellow, and pale aubergine with extensive traces of thin gilding.

The silver-gilt, domed, hinged cover is attached to a band, engraved in the German floral style, encircling the loop handle; a stopper in the bird's beak is connected by a chain to a plain band around the bird's neck; and the oval base is decorated with engraved rope twists and leaves.

A virtually identical ewer, in the Staatliche Porzellansammlung, Dresden, Germany, appears in the Dresden Kunstkammer inventory from 1595.[1] A wine ewer shaped like a phoenix and another like a crayfish, both enameled on the biscuit, were presented by the grand duke Ferdinand I of Tuscany to the elector Christian I of Saxony in 1590.[2] Together with a crayfish or lobster ewer, examples of which are in the Hainhofer Cabinet at Uppsala, Sweden, a collection completed in 1628,[3] and the Rijksmuseum, Amsterdam,[4] these porcelains form a small group of wares exported to the West toward the end of the Ming dynasty. Having soft lead-silicate glazes enameled on the biscuit, these Ming ceramics are predecessors of the many figures and groups from the Kangxi reign decorated in this technique with the addition of gilding.

The silver-gilt oval foot mount, possibly dating from the beginning of the seventeenth century, is attributed to Friedrich Hillebrand, a prominent goldsmith from Nuremberg, who became a *Meister* (master) in 1580 and died in 1608. Hillebrand specialized in creating precious vessels in the shapes of birds, often incorporating mother-of-pearl inlays and nautilus shells in his designs.[5] Stamped on the rope twists of the oval foot mount are Hillebrand's initials in a rectangle, and underneath the foot ring is an unidentified eight-pointed star punch, as recorded by Marc Rosenberg on three sixteenth- and seventeenth-century *Hostiendose,* or containers for the Host, in the treasury of the Johanneskirche, Schweinfurt, Germany.[6]

1. Friedrich Reichel, *Schätze Chinas aus Museen der DDR,* Roemer- und Pelizaeus-Museum, Hildesheim, 1990, p. 262, no. 157, documenting the ewer in the 1595 Dresden inventory: "I Pocal von Porcellana wie ein Drache verguldet, auch grün und blau geferbett" (one pitcher [German derivative of Italian *bocale,* or pitcher?] of porcelain as a gilded dragon [meaning phoenix?], colored in green and blue). See also R. L. Hobson, *The Wares of the Ming Dynasty,* New York, 1923, p. 147, pl. 36, dating the ewer as in the Dresden inventory before 1640. As illustrated in Reichel, the Dresden example is broken across the neck and has lost both its mounts and gilding.

2. Reichel, p. 262: "Ahn Italianischenn Trinck und andern Geschirrenn, welche Anno 1590 von dem Hertzogenn von Florentz sind vorehret worden" (An Italian drink [ewer] and other crockery, which in 1590 was presented respectfully by the duke of Florence). As Reichel documents, Chinese porcelains are recorded in Florence by 1487, when the Egyptian sultan gave a number of ceramics to Lorenzo de' Medici. See also L. Reidemeister, "Eine Schenkung chinesischer Porzellane aus dem Ende des 16. Jahrhunderts," *Ostasiatische Zeitschift,* vol. IX (1933), p. 12.

3. Hobson, p. 147. Hobson believed that these related works originated from one factory and were brought to Europe at the same time.

4. See *Asiatic Art in the Rijksmuseum, Amsterdam,* ed. Pauline Lunsingh Scheurleer, Amsterdam, 1985, p. 80, fig. 63, for another example of the crayfish or lobster ewer.

5. Marc Rosenberg, *Deutschland, N–Z,* vol. III of *Der Goldschmiede Merkzeichen,* Frankfurt am Main, 1925, pp. 132–34.

6. Rosenberg, *Ausland und Byzanz,* vol. IV, 1928, p. 603.

Provenance [Duveen, New York (as having "mounts of the Ming period")]; Taft collection, Apr. 23, 1910.

Exhibition Cincinnati, Taft Museum, *Ming to Ch'ing: Imperial Objects and Textiles, Masterpieces of Chinese Furniture,* Feb. 12–June 30, 1975.

Literature *Catalogue of the Taft Museum,* Cincinnati, 1939 and 1958, no. 289.

1931.18

Vase

Ming dynasty (1368–1644), sixteenth century
Stoneware, H. 38.1 cm (15 in.)
Unmarked

This baluster vase of the *fahua,* or raised colors, type with elephant-head handles attached to the tall trumpet neck has an aubergine ground slip outlined with full-blown white lotus among leaves and water weeds in bright turquoise.

Also known as the cloisonné technique, *fahua* decorations are delineated by thin clay outlines that create shallow reliefs to control the flow of the polychrome glazes during firing. Characteristic of these wares are the streaked and crackled glazes. Stoneware examples such as the three at the Taft (see the following entries), with typical aubergine or turquoise background colors over slightly coarse brown clay, were probably made at kilns throughout China for local sale and may have been produced somewhat earlier in the Ming dynasty.[1]

1. Suzanne G. Valenstein, *A Handbook of Chinese Ceramics,* New York, 1989, pp. 177–78.

1931.22

Provenance Robert H. Benson, Park Lane and Buckhurst Park, Sussex (sale, Christie's, London, July 2, 1924, no. 121, although with French ormolu mounts); [Parish-Watson, New York]; Taft collection, Oct. 30, 1924.

Literature *Catalogue of the Taft Museum,* Cincinnati, 1939 and 1958, no. 298.

1931.22

Vase

Ming dynasty (1368–1644), sixteenth or seventeenth century
Stoneware, H. 41.9 cm (16½ in.)
Unmarked

This tall pear-shaped vase of the *fahua,* or raised colors, type, with bisquit lion masks set on the neck has a pale turquoise

1931.23

1931.21

ground with applied molded and modeled butterflies and bees hovering above flowering chrysanthemums in aubergine and darker blue.

Provenance Robert H. Benson, Park Lane and Buckhurst Park, Sussex (sale, Christie's, London, July 1, 1924, no. 23); [Parish-Watson, New York]; Taft collection, Oct. 30, 1924.

Literature *Fortune* (July 1931), p. 69 (color ill.); *Catalogue of the Taft Museum,* Cincinnati, 1939 and 1958, no. 302.

1931.23

Vase

Ming dynasty (1368–1644), 1600–1644
Stoneware, H. 41.3 cm (16¼ in.)
Unmarked

This pear-shaped vase of the *fahua,* or raised colors, type has a violet-purple-glaze ground with applied molded and modeled bees hovering over flowering chrysanthemums. The handles are long-tailed *guilong,* or serpentine dragons, clambering toward the trumpet neck.

Provenance J. Pierpont Morgan, New York (in 1911); Robert H. Benson, Park Lane and Buckhurst Park, Sussex (sale, Christie's, London, July 1, 1924, no. 34); [Parish-Watson, New York]; Taft collection, Oct. 30, 1924.

Exhibition Cincinnati, Taft Museum, *Ming to Ch'ing: Imperial Objects and Textiles, Masterpieces of Chinese Furniture,* Feb. 12–June 30, 1975.

Literature J. Pierpont Morgan, *Catalogue of the Morgan Collection of Chinese Porcelains,* vol. II, New York, 1911, pl. LXXXI; R. L. Hobson, *The Wares of the Ming Dynasty,* New York, 1923, pl. 52, fig. 1; *Fortune* (July 1931), p. 69 (color ill.); *Catalogue of the Taft Museum,* Cincinnati, 1939 and 1958, no. 291.

1931.21

1931.66, 70

Two Wine Cups

Ming dynasty (1368–1644), 1630–44
Porcelain, DIAM. (each) 8.9 cm (3½ in.)
Unmarked unglazed bases

These reticulated white wine cups have short foot rings and flaring lips. Each is decorated with five gilded relief roundels of two figures, probably representing Daoist Immortals, set on cash-pattern *linglong,* or openwork, grounds between underglaze blue bands of foliate lappets. One has a diaper pattern below the unglazed lip; the other, a dentil pattern.

Each is engraved with a line for the sprung-metal sheet liners. Silver liners were often used in wine cups of the period.

Provenance [Duveen, New York]; Taft collection, Nov. 5, 1903.

Literature John Getz, *A Catalogue of Chinese Porcelains Collected by Mr. and Mrs. Charles P. Taft,* New York, 1904, nos. 31–32; *Catalogue of the Taft Museum,* Cincinnati, 1939 and 1958, nos. 62, 64.

1931.66, 1931.70

Qing Dynasty Blue-and-White

Oviform Jar with Domed Cover

Kangxi reign (Qing dynasty), 1662–1722
Porcelain, H. 26.4 x DIAM. 20.9 cm (10⅜ x 8¼ in.)
Unmarked

This blue-and-white broad oviform storage jar with domed cover and tapering foot ring is reserved in white with four flowering prunus branches ascending and descending on a brilliant washed sapphire blue cracked-ice ground. The unglazed neck is decorated with a dentil border. The foot ring is unglazed with a plain glazed base.

This type of oviform jar, also referred to as a "prunus," "hawthorn," or "ginger jar" (see 1931.15), was considered by scholars and dealers alike at the beginning of the twentieth century as the finest type of Chinese blue-and-white porcelain ever made. The best of the Yuan dynasty (1271–1368) and early Ming dynasty (1368–1644) blue-and-white ceramics as well as those from all periods made especially for imperial use, however, are currently considered superior.

This type of covered jar, according to R. L. Hobson, was used by the Chinese to send "gifts of fragrant tea or sweetmeats to

1931.11

1931.11 top

1931.15 top

their friends at the New Year."[1] The design suggests the passing of winter with the breaking up of ice and the flowering of the prunus. The prunus, or *Prunus mume,* a Chinese and Japanese species of plum tree, is a popular motif in Chinese art since its name, *mei hua,* includes a homophone for beauty, *mei.*

1. R. L. Hobson, *The Later Ceramic Wares of China,* London, 1924, p. 14.

Provenance James W. Ellsworth; [Parish-Watson, New York (according to original invoice, "cover repaired" and "as far as our records show there are 44 pieces of this quality known")]; Taft collection, Nov. 9, 1923.

Literature *Catalogue of the Taft Museum,* Cincinnati, 1939 and 1958, no. 65; Anthony Derham, "Blue-and-White at a Price," *Apollo,* n.s., vol. CXXVIII, no. 322 (Dec. 1988), pp. 406–7, fig. 1; David Torbet Johnson, "Taft Museum," *Ventura,* vol. IV, no. 16 (June–Aug. 1991), p. 140 (ill.).

1931.11

Oviform Jar with Domed Cover

Kangxi reign (Qing dynasty), 1662–1722
Porcelain, H. 24.5 X DIAM. 19.8 cm (9⅝ x 7⅞ in.)
Unmarked; later diamond-engraved collector's marks

This blue-and-white broad oviform storage jar with domed cover and tapering foot ring is reserved in white with four flowering prunus branches ascending and descending on a brilliant washed sapphire blue cracked-ice ground. The unglazed neck is decorated with a dentil border. The foot ring is unglazed with a plain glazed base (see 1931.11).

Provenance [Duveen, New York (according to original invoice, "superb and rare" and "of this quality there are only 19 known in the world")]; Taft collection, Apr. 28, 1902.

Literature John Getz, *A Catalogue of Chinese Porcelains Collected by Mr. and Mrs. Charles P. Taft,* New York, 1904, no. 22; *Catalogue of the Taft Museum,* Cincinnati, 1939 and 1958, no. 71; Anthony Derham, "Blue-and-White at a Price," *Apollo,* n.s., vol. CXXVIII, no. 322 (Dec. 1988), pp. 406–7, pl. II.

1931.15

1931.15

1931.58

Oviform Jar with Domed Cover

Kangxi reign (Qing dynasty), 1662–1722
Porcelain, H. 13 cm (5⅛ in.)
Mark: underglaze blue artemisia leaf

This blue-and-white broad oviform jar with domed cover and short flaring base is painted with bold stylized flowering lotus and leafy branch scrolls. The cover is decorated en suite and has a small seated Buddhistic lion finial.

The lotus flower, also referred to as *hehua* or *lianhua,* is a Chinese symbol for marriage. Since *he* is a homophone for "harmony" and *lian* for "continuous," the design decorating this jar probably represents a wish for domestic happiness.[1]

1. Terese Tse Bartholomew, *Myths and Rebuses in Chinese Art,* exh. cat., Asian Art Museum of San Francisco, 1988, n.p.

Provenance [Duveen, New York]; Taft collection, Apr. 28, 1902.

Literature John Getz, *A Catalogue of Chinese Porcelains Collected by Mr. and Mrs. Charles P. Taft,* New York, 1904, no. 5; *Catalogue of the Taft Museum,* Cincinnati, 1939 and 1958, no. 66.

1931.58

Pair of Oviform Jars

Kangxi reign (Qing dynasty), 1662–1722
Porcelain, H. (each) 13.7 cm (5⅜ in.)
Mark: underglaze blue ribboned artemisia leaf within double ring

This pair of blue-and-white oviform jars set on short flaring bases is painted with flowers incorporating *lingzhi* heads among long leafy scrolls. Both jars are missing small shallow domed covers (see 1931.52).

The *lingzhi* (*Polyporus lucidus*), a dark, woody fungus that grows at the bases of trees in southern China, is highly prized by the Chinese as the fungus of immortality. "As the fungus resembles the *ruyi* scepter," Terese Tse Bartholomew notes in her explanation of Chinese myths, "it has come to represent the *ruyi* and is thus a wish-fulfilling as well as a longevity symbol."[1]

1931.58 detail of mark

1931.54 detail of mark

1931.50, 54

1. Terese Tse Bartholomew, *Myths and Rebuses in Chinese Art*, exh. cat., Asian Art Museum of San Francisco, 1988, n.p.

Provenance [Duveen, New York]; Taft collection, June 14, 1902.

Literature John Getz, *A Catalogue of Chinese Porcelains Collected by Mr. and Mrs. Charles P. Taft*, New York, 1904, no. 7 (formerly with "low, flat covers"); *Catalogue of the Taft Museum*, Cincinnati, 1939 and 1958, nos. 55, 57.

1931.50, 1931.54

Oviform Jar with Cover

Kangxi reign (Qing dynasty), 1662–1722
Porcelain, H. 16.2 cm (6⅜ in.)
Mark: underglaze blue ribboned artemisia leaf within double ring

This blue-and-white oviform jar with shallow domed cover and short flaring base is painted with flowers incorporating *lingzhi* heads among long leafy scrolls, formerly known as "tiger lily" scrolls (see 1931.50, 54).

Provenance [Duveen, New York]; Taft collection, June 14, 1902.

Literature John Getz, *A Catalogue of Chinese Porcelains Collected by Mr. and Mrs. Charles P. Taft*, New York, 1904, no. 6; *Catalogue of the Taft Museum*, Cincinnati, 1939 and 1958, no. 63.

1931.52

1931.52

1931.65, 71

Pair of Cylindrical Jars with Domed Covers

Kangxi reign (Qing dynasty), 1662–1722
Porcelain, H. (each) 19.6 cm (7¾ in.)
Mark: underglaze blue double ring

This pair of blue-and-white cylindrical jars with shallow domed covers and short foot rings is painted en suite with a foliate-shaped panel of chrysanthemums, a quatrefoil panel of wild pinks, and a fan-shaped panel of cockscomb, all on washed cracked-ice-pattern grounds with scattered white prunus flowers. The covers have plain blue bud finials.

1931.65 detail of mark

Provenance [Duveen, New York]; Taft collection, June 14, 1902.

Exhibition Cincinnati, Taft Museum [also Flint, Mich., and Muncie, Ind.], *China in 1700: Kangxi Porcelains at the Taft Museum*, Sept. 8, 1988–Sept. 17, 1989 (cat. by Sheila Keppel, no. 71 [1931.65]).

Literature John Getz, *A Catalogue of Chinese Porcelains Collected by Mr. and Mrs. Charles P. Taft*, New York, 1904, no. 2; *Catalogue of the Taft Museum*, Cincinnati, 1939 and 1958, nos. 49, 76.

1931.65, 1931.71

Beaker Vase

Kangxi reign (Qing dynasty), 1662–1722
Porcelain, H. 23.5 cm (9¼ in.)
Mark: underglaze blue double ring

The shape of this blue-and-white beaker vase is derived from the archaic bronze *gu* with a slightly raised band between the flaring base and trumpet mouth. It is painted with flowering prunus branches reserved in white on a washed blue cracked-ice-pattern ground.

Provenance [Duveen, New York]; Taft collection, Apr. 18, 1902.

1931.13

1931.188, 190

Literature John Getz, *A Catalogue of Chinese Porcelains Collected by Mr. and Mrs. Charles P. Taft,* New York, 1904, no. 1; *Catalogue of the Taft Museum,* Cincinnati, 1939 and 1958, no. 52.

1931.13

Pair of Beaker Vases

Kangxi reign (Qing dynasty), 1662–1722
Porcelain, H. (each) 43.5 cm (17⅛ in.)
Mark: underglaze blue ribboned artemisia leaf within double ring

This pair of blue-and-white beaker vases has flaring bases, slightly bulbous central sections, and trumpet necks. The vases are molded with lotus-petal panels, which are painted alternately with flowering plants and ladies at elegant pastimes in four tiers: with children on the top section; with jardinieres of flowering plants on low tables and ladies playing a guitar and flute on the second section; with flowering plants and ladies dancing to cymbals on the convex section; and with ladies caressing birds and a rabbit on the fourth section. The grounds are decorated with flower sprays and bands of hatched patterns.

Dutch traders disparagingly referred to the slender and graceful Chinese women depicted on these beaker vases as *Lange Lijsen,* or "long stupids" (see 1931.187, 191, and 189, pp. 584–85). *Lange Lijsen* was later anglicized in England and America to the somewhat more acceptable "Long Elizas." In China these long-limbed figures are known as *meiren.*

1931.188 detail of mark

In John Getz's catalogue of the Taft porcelain collection (1904) and in the handbook to the Taft Museum collections (1939 and 1958), this pair of beaker vases and the following three baluster vases with domed covers are described as a *garniture de cheminée,* or chimney garniture. The inconsistencies in the underglaze blue decorations, individual dimensions, and underglaze marks, however, indicate that the porcelains are not a matching garniture.

1931.191, 187

A similar set of three baluster and two beaker vases, decorated with underglaze blue floral designs rather than figures, is listed in the Danish royal inventory of 1701 (now in the Nationalmuseet, department of ethnography, Copenhagen, Denmark, inv. no. EBc 169–72).[1] During the late seventeenth century, the Dutch fashion for ornamental chimney decorations, popularized by the French architect and designer Daniel Marot, spread to the English, German, and Danish royal courts. European collectors created garnitures, probably based on the Chinese family altar sets, from the large numbers of these wares that were being exported to the West. As a result the individual components of these sets are sometimes slightly mismatched, as in the case of the Taft examples.

1. Michel Beurdeley and Guy Raindre, *Qing Porcelains: Famille Verte, Famille Rose, 1644–1912*, trans. Charlotte Chesney, New York, 1987, p. 45.

Provenance [Duveen, New York]; Taft collection, Dec. 12, 1902.

Literature John Getz, *A Catalogue of Chinese Porcelains Collected by Mr. and Mrs. Charles P. Taft*, New York, 1904, no. 17; Margaret Kremers, "A 'Long Eliza' Garniture in the Taft Museum," *Bulletin of the Cincinnati Art Museum*, vol. VIII, no. 2 (Apr. 1937), pp. 40–48 (both ill.); *Catalogue of the Taft Museum*, Cincinnati, 1939 and 1958, nos. 68, 70.

1931.188, 1931.190

Pair of Baluster Vases with Covers

Kangxi reign (Qing dynasty), 1662–1722
Porcelain, H. (each) 49.5 cm (19½ in.)
Mark: underglaze blue six-character Chenghua reign mark (1465–87); actually of the Kangxi period

Each of this pair of blue-and-white, tall, slender baluster vases and covers is molded with overlapping lotus-petal panels painted on the central band with mounted huntsmen-warriors above a band of panels with jardinieres of plants on tables alternating with lady musicians. The upper band is painted with beautiful women dancing among scattered flower sprays; the necks, with flowering branches of chrysanthemum, prunus, morning glory, tiger lily, and tree peony; the covers, painted en suite with lotus-bud finials.

The presence of this Ming mark on some Kangxi ceramics may be explained by the legislation of 1677 that forbade the use of the Kangxi *nianhao,* or year-name mark of an emperor's reign, on nonimperial wares. In addition, the veneration of ceramics produced during the Ming dynasty reigns of the Xuande emperor (1426–35) and the Chenghua emperor (1465–87) led to the widespread use of their reign marks on Kangxi-period porcelains, whether decorated in the Ming styles or not.

Provenance [Duveen, New York]; Taft collection, Dec. 12, 1902.

Literature John Getz, *A Catalogue of Chinese Porcelains Collected by Mr. and Mrs. Charles P. Taft,* New York, 1904, no. 18; Margaret Kremers, "A 'Long Eliza' Garniture in the Taft Museum," *Bulletin of the Cincinnati Art Museum,* vol. VIII, no. 2 (Apr. 1937), pp. 40–48; *Catalogue of the Taft Museum,* Cincinnati, 1939 and 1958, nos. 67, 71.

1931.187, 1931.191

1931.187 detail of mark

Baluster Vase with Cover

Kangxi reign (Qing dynasty), 1662–1722
Porcelain, H. 45.8 cm (18 in.)
Mark: underglaze blue ribboned artemisia leaf

This blue-and-white slender baluster vase with cover is molded with overlapping lotus-petal panels painted alternately with elegant ladies, who play instruments or are accompanied by children, and jardinieres of flowering plants on low tables. The grounds are decorated with scattered flower sprays and branches on the neck. The domed cover is painted en suite and has a plain knob finial.

Provenance [Duveen, New York]; Taft collection, Dec. 12, 1902.

Literature John Getz, *A Catalogue of Chinese Porcelains Collected by Mr. and Mrs. Charles P. Taft,* New York, 1904, no. 16; Margaret Kremers, "A 'Long Eliza' Garniture in the Taft Museum," *Bulletin of the Cincinnati Art Museum,* vol. VIII, no. 2 (Apr. 1937), pp. 40–48 (ill.); *Catalogue of the Taft Museum,* Cincinnati, 1939 and 1958, no. 69.

1931.189

1931.189

1931.194

Baluster Vase

Kangxi reign (Qing dynasty), 1662–1722
Porcelain, H. 45.7 cm (18 in.)
Unmarked

This blue-and-white vase with a baluster body and wide trumpet neck is painted with bands of tasseled knotting above flowering tree peony and chrysanthemum scrolls divided by bands of painted tablet-shaped lappets, *ruyi* heads, and zigzags.

Provenance [Duveen, New York]; Taft collection, Dec. 12, 1902.
Literature John Getz, *A Catalogue of Chinese Porcelains Collected by Mr. and Mrs. Charles P. Taft*, New York, 1904, no. 21; *Catalogue of the Taft Museum*, Cincinnati, 1939 and 1958, no. 79.

1931.194

Baluster Vase

Kangxi reign (Qing dynasty), ca. 1700
Porcelain, H. 77.5 cm (30½ in.)
Unmarked

This massive blue-and-white baluster vase with trumpet neck is painted with an elaborate scene of scholar-officials looking from a second-floor pavilion terrace at elegant ladies riding out through a trellised arbor. Two male figures stand behind the trellis. The neck is decorated with a girl reading to an official tutor at a desk and an elderly scholar sitting between fan and lantern bearers before a screen.

Probably derived from the *Yang Jia Jiang,* or *The Generals of the Yang Family,* written by Yong Damu (whose other names are Zhonggu and Aufeng) during the Ming dynasty (1368–1644), this scene depicts northern Song dynasty (960–1127) women from the Yang family training for mounted combat against Liao dynasty (907–1125) invaders from Manchuria. The emphasis in this subject on loyalty to and sacrifice for the reigning Song em-

1931.138 the Yang family generals

1931.138 scholar-officials observing women training

1931.138 Yang family women training for mounted combat

peror — even after the Yang family males were depleted in earlier battles — illustrates one of the Kangxi emperor's "uses of the past."[1] Mythical or historical scenes such as this one were used as political propaganda to consolidate the power base of the Kangxi emperor's foreign Manchu dynasty and to stave off further protests from supplanted Ming dynasty loyalists.

1. Sheila Keppel, *China in 1700: Kangxi Porcelains at the Taft Museum,* exh. cat., Cincinnati, 1988, pp. 12–13.

Provenance Taft collection, after 1904.

Exhibitions Cincinnati, Taft Museum, *Ming to Ch'ing: Imperial Objects and Textiles, Masterpieces of Chinese Furniture,* Feb. 12–June 30, 1975; Cincinnati, Taft Museum [also Flint, Mich., and Muncie, Ind.], *China in 1700: Kangxi Porcelains at the Taft Museum,* Sept. 8, 1988–Sept. 17, 1989 (cat. by Sheila Keppel, no. 48).

Literature *Catalogue of the Taft Museum,* Cincinnati, 1939 and 1958, no. 244.

1931.138

Baluster Vase

Kangxi reign (Qing dynasty), ca. 1700
Porcelain, H. 70.5 cm (27¾ in.)
Unmarked

This blue-and-white baluster vase with tall trumpet neck is painted in a brilliant washed blue with an allover pattern of formal flowering lotus scrolls. Bands of flowered zigzags decorate the vase at the base and below the lip.

The statement on the Duveen invoice that this vase came from the Summer Palace may be true. In the inventory taken by Major Noel du Boulay when he was commandant of the Summer Palace in 1900–1901, the first item listed under "K'ang Hsi

1931.157

1931.68

(1661–1722)" is "Pair of large vases; blue flowers."[1] The particular lotus pattern on this vase was also copied during the reign of the Guangxu emperor (1875–1908) for the dowager empress to use in the Summer Palace.

1. Anthony du Boulay, "The Summer Palace, Beijing, 1900: An Inventory by Noel du Boulay, Commandant, 1900–1901," *Transactions of the Oriental Ceramic Society* (1990–91), p. 98.

Provenance Hebu P. Bishop; [Duveen, New York (as "from the looting of the Summer Palace, Peking, 1860")]; Taft collection, Apr. 19, 1906.

Exhibitions Cincinnati, Taft Museum, *Ming to Ch'ing: Imperial Objects and Textiles, Masterpieces of Chinese Furniture,* Feb. 12–June 30, 1975; Cincinnati, Taft Museum [also Flint, Mich., and Muncie, Ind.], *China in 1700: Kangxi Porcelains at the Taft Museum,* Sept. 8, 1988–Sept. 17, 1989 (cat. by Sheila Keppel, no. 68).

Literature *Catalogue of the Taft Museum,* Cincinnati, 1939 and 1958, no. 274.

1931.157

Rouleau Vase

Kangxi reign (Qing dynasty), 1662–1722
Porcelain, H. 27.9 cm (11 in.)
Mark: underglaze blue double ring

This blue-and-white rouleau vase with a short flaring neck is painted with bands of formal flower and leafy branch scrolls, *guilong* (serpentine dragons) among leaves reserved in white on a washed blue ground, and *ruyi* lappet panels of lotus flowers. The neck is painted with overlapping leaves.

Provenance [Duveen, New York]; Taft collection, Dec. 12, 1902.

Literature John Getz, *A Catalogue of Chinese Porcelains Collected by Mr. and Mrs. Charles P. Taft,* New York, 1904, no. 15; *Catalogue of the Taft Museum,* Cincinnati, 1939 and 1958, no. 56.

1931.68

Rouleau Vase

Kangxi reign (Qing dynasty), 1662–1722
Porcelain, H. 45.7 cm (18 in.)
Unmarked

1931.193 Chang'e receiving new examination candidate

This blue-and-white rouleau vase is painted on the body with a scholar-official approaching a court lady seated in front of a large garden screen and surrounded by her attendants. Two female lantern bearers stand to one side on the terrace. A desk is set with scholar's objects, and a draped yoke-back chair is behind the screen.

The subject of this vase has been identified as Chang'e receiving a newly graduated civil-service examination candidate in the Guang-han gong (Palace of the Far-Reaching Cold, or Moon Palace).[1] Chang'e, wife of the legendary chieftain Hou Yi (ca. 2500 B.C.), stole the elixir of immortality from her husband, who had obtained it from Xi Wangmu, Queen Mother of the West, and fled with the elixir to the moon. The gods changed Chang'e into a toad or a hare, whose outline the Chinese see on the surface of the moon.[2] Chang'e, the moon goddess, traditionally greets young scholars who have passed the national civil-service examinations by offering a branch of the flowering cassia tree, which is symbolic of success in this important test. Porcelains decorated with subjects such as this would have been marketed to the literati class of scholar-officials during the seventeenth century.

This rouleau vase is an outstanding example of the classic Kangxi blue-and-white style: the decoration covers the entire body of the vase and is executed in three shades of cobalt blue wash and fine lines.

1. Sheila Keppel, *China in 1700: Kangxi Porcelains at the Taft Museum,* exh. cat., Cincinnati, 1988, p. 13, and Wolfram Eberhard, *A Dictionary of Chinese Symbols,* trans. G. L. Campbell, London, 1991, p. 60.

2. C. A. S. Williams, *Outlines of Chinese Symbolism and Art Motives,* New York, 1976, p. 403.

Provenance Taft collection, by 1904.

Exhibition Cincinnati, Taft Museum [also Flint, Mich., and Muncie, Ind.], *China in 1700: Kangxi Porcelains at the Taft Museum,* Sept. 8, 1988–Sept. 17, 1989 (cat. by Sheila Keppel, no. 49).

Literature John Getz, *A Catalogue of Chinese Porcelains Collected by Mr. and Mrs. Charles P. Taft,* New York, 1904, no. 20; *Catalogue of the Taft Museum,* Cincinnati, 1939 and 1958, no. 51.

1931.193

1931.62

Bottle Vase

Kangxi reign (Qing dynasty), 1662–1722
Porcelain, H. 25.7 cm (10⅛ in.)
Mark: underglaze blue double ring

This blue-and-white pear-shaped bottle vase is painted with six vertical panels alternately decorated with the *babao* (Eight Precious Things), ladies seated by vases in subsidiary fan-shaped panels, and *bogu* (the Hundred Antiques, or scholar's objects).

The tall slender neck, divided into three bands by hatched ornament, has stiff leaves in the center and scattered flower heads above and below. The slightly flared lip and shoulder are decorated with shaped lappets.

Provenance [Duveen, New York]; Taft collection, Dec. 12, 1902.

Literature John Getz, *A Catalogue of Chinese Porcelains Collected by Mr. and Mrs. Charles P. Taft,* New York, 1904, no. 4; *Catalogue of the Taft Museum,* Cincinnati, 1939 and 1958, no. 78.

1931.62

Pair of Bud Vases

Kangxi reign (Qing dynasty), ca. 1680–1700
Porcelain: 1931.61, H. 16.2 cm (6⅜ in.); 1931.63, H. 15.9 cm (6¼ in.)
Unmarked

Each of these blue-and-white bud vases has a flattened pear-shaped body, a flaring foot ring, and a tall slender neck. Each is painted with a wide band of stylized lotus among leafy branches below tall overlapping leaves and bands of petals and flower heads at the lips.

The random lichen spotting on the foot rings is often characteristic of the Transitional Period (ca. 1644–75), but the quality of manufacture suggests an origin during the middle years of the reign of the Kangxi emperor.

Provenance [Probably Duveen, New York]; Taft collection, by 1904.

Literature John Getz, *A Catalogue of Chinese Porcelains Collected by Mr. and Mrs. Charles P. Taft,* New York, 1904, no. 12; *Catalogue of the Taft Museum,* Cincinnati, 1939 and 1958, nos. 53, 59.

1931.61, 1931.63

Pair of Pear-shaped Vases

Kangxi reign (Qing dynasty), 1662–1722
Porcelain, H. (each) 26 cm (10¼ in.)
Mark: underglaze blue peony spray

Each of these two blue-and-white pear-shaped vases with flaring foot rings and tall slender necks is painted with two horned and leafy-tailed dragons chasing flaming pearls among flames and clouds. The dragons are positioned above breaking waves, and their necks are twisted to look up at flower sprays below bands of strapwork, waves, and stiff leaves.

The flaming pearl is a nearly constant accessory of the dragon in Chinese art. It has been variously described as representing the sun, the moon, the *yin yang* symbol of the dual forces of nature, and the pearl of potentiality.[1] A pearl entwined with a fillet, or ribbon, is one of the *babao,* or Eight Precious Things, and a symbol of good omens.

1. C. A. S. Williams, *Outlines of Chinese Symbolism and Art Motives,* New York, 1976, p. 138.

Provenance [Duveen, New York]; Taft collection, Dec. 12, 1902.

1931.61, 63

1931.60, 64

1931.60 detail of mark

Exhibition Cincinnati, Taft Museum [also Flint, Mich., and Muncie, Ind.], *China in 1700: Kangxi Porcelains at the Taft Museum*, Sept. 8, 1988–Sept. 17, 1989 (cat. by Sheila Keppel, no. 4 [1931.64]).

Literature John Getz, *A Catalogue of Chinese Porcelains Collected by Mr. and Mrs. Charles P. Taft*, New York, 1904, no. 14; *Catalogue of the Taft Museum*, Cincinnati, 1939 and 1958, nos. 54, 58.

1931.60, 1931.64

Pair of Pear-shaped Bottles

Kangxi reign (Qing dynasty), 1662–1722
Porcelain, H. (each) 19 cm (7½ in.)
Mark: underglaze blue artemisia leaf

1931.51, 53

Each of these blue-and-white pear-shaped bottles with short, slightly flaring foot rings and slender necks is painted with joined panels of lotus scrolls, reserved in white on washed blue grounds between bands of overlapping petals with scattered flower heads on the white grounds between. The necks are decorated with small foliage-filled quatrefoil panels on brocaded grounds and with hatched bands.[1]

1. An identical set of pear-shaped bottles is illustrated in Edgar Gorer, *Catalogue of the Collection of Old Chinese Porcelains Formed by Richard Bennett, Esq., Thornby Hall, Northampton,* London, n.d., p. 12, no. 55, pl. 55.

Provenance [Duveen, New York]; Taft collection, Apr. 28, 1902.

Literature John Getz, *A Catalogue of Chinese Porcelains Collected by Mr. and Mrs. Charles P. Taft,* New York, 1904, no. 13; *Catalogue of the Taft Museum,* Cincinnati, 1939 and 1958, nos. 75, 77.

1931.51, 1931.53

Pair of Pear-shaped Bottles

Kangxi reign (Qing dynasty), 1662–1722
Porcelain, H. (each) 19 cm (7½ in.)
Unmarked

Each of this pair of blue-and-white pear-shaped bottles is painted with a peasant punting a sampan toward two scholars standing at the lakeside below pavilions set among trees and rocks. The slender necks are decorated with hatched bands at the lips.

The theme of scholars in nature was derived from landscape painting, perhaps arriving at Jingdezhen via wood-block-printed books. The motif was intended to appeal to the domestic market when trade routes were blocked, in this case, during the late Transitional Period (ca. 1644–75).[1]

1. I gratefully acknowledge Sheila Keppel's assistance with identifying this theme.

Provenance [Duveen, New York]; Taft collection, Dec. 12, 1902.

Exhibition Cincinnati, Taft Museum [also Flint, Mich., and Muncie, Ind.], *China in 1700: Kangxi Porcelains at the Taft Museum,* Sept. 8, 1988–Sept. 17, 1989 (cat. by Sheila Keppel, no. 59 [1931.59]).

Literature John Getz, *A Catalogue of Chinese Porcelains Collected by Mr. and Mrs. Charles P. Taft,* New York, 1904, no. 3; *Catalogue of the Taft Museum,* Cincinnati, 1939 and 1958, nos. 48, 50.

1931.55, 1931.59

Teapot

Kangxi reign (Qing Dynasty), 1662–1722
Porcelain, H. 15.9 cm (6¼ in.)
Unmarked

This blue-and-white tapering oviform teapot with domed cover is molded and carved with a rope net in low relief on the body, whereas the loop handle and tall spout are molded as rope twists. The teapot is painted with a washed blue ground leaving sprays of chrysanthemum and lotus in white. The cover is similarly painted and decorated with a knot finial and rope border.

1931.55, 59

1931.67

Provenance [Duveen, New York]; Taft collection, Dec. 12, 1902.

Exhibition Dayton Art Institute, Ohio, *Made in China: Chinese Export Ware,* Jan. 17–Mar. 1, 1987.

Literature John Getz, *A Catalogue of Chinese Porcelains Collected by Mr. and Mrs. Charles P. Taft,* New York, 1904, no. 10; *Catalogue of the Taft Museum,* Cincinnati, 1939 and 1958, no. 45 (ill.).

1931.67

Teapot

Kangxi reign (Qing dynasty), 1662–1722
Porcelain, H. 16.8 cm (6⅝ in.)
Unmarked

This blue-and-white globular teapot with a small flat cover has a tall, squared loop handle and short spout molded as bamboo. The body of the teapot is painted with panels of vases, baskets, and jardinieres filled with branches of *lingzhi* fungus, grasses, pinks, lotus, and peony. The cover is decorated with berried branches and chrysanthemums growing from rockwork.

Provenance [Duveen, New York]; Taft collection, Apr. 28, 1902.

Literature John Getz, *A Catalogue of Chinese Porcelains Collected by Mr. and Mrs. Charles P. Taft,* New York, 1904, no. 11; *Catalogue of the Taft Museum,* Cincinnati, 1939 and 1958, no. 72.

1931.69

1931.69

1931.56

Teapot

Kangxi reign (Qing dynasty), 1662–1722
Porcelain, H. 10.8 cm (4¼ in.)
Mark: underglaze blue ribboned jewel within double ring

This blue-and-white globular teapot has a squared loop handle and a short curved, tapering spout. The body is reserved in white with two small boys running and holding flowering peony scrolls on a washed blue ground; the handle and spout are decorated with flower heads. The cover is period but possibly from a different pot since the glaze, a very pale blue, is inconsistent with the decoration on the body of the pot.

Provenance [Duveen, New York]; Taft collection, Nov. 29, 1903.

Literature John Getz, *A Catalogue of Chinese Porcelains Collected by Mr. and Mrs. Charles P. Taft,* New York, 1904, no. 9; *Catalogue of the Taft Museum,* Cincinnati, 1939 and 1958, no. 60.

1931.56

Meiping

Yongzheng reign (Qing dynasty), 1723–35
Soft-paste porcelain, H. 17.8 cm (7 in.)
Unmarked

This soft-paste porcelain blue-and-white *meiping* is painted in outlined wash with fruiting branches of pomegranate, peach, and Buddha-hand citron between bands of stiff leaves, lappets, and foliage scrolls all under a lightly stained, typically crackled clear glaze.

The so-called Chinese soft-paste porcelain is made from a clay incorporating *huashi* ("slippery stone") to replace the kaolin in the manufacture.

The Buddha-hand citron, also known as the finger citrus, or *Citrus medica* var. *sarcodactylis,* is a rebus for blessings. According to Terese Tse Bartholomew, the shape of this fruit recalls the fingers of Buddha and in China is called *foshou,* which is nearly homophonous with "blessings" and "longevity." The grouping of pomegranates, peaches, and Buddha-hand citrons together is known as *sanduo,* or the Three Plenties, a wish for an abundance of offspring, longevity, and blessings.[1]

1. Terese Tse Bartholomew, *Myths and Rebuses in Chinese Art,* exh. cat., Asian Art Museum of San Francisco, 1988, n.p.

Provenance Taft collection, after 1904.

Exhibition Cincinnati, Taft Museum [also Flint, Mich., and Muncie, Ind.], *China in 1700: Kangxi Porcelains at the Taft Museum,* Sept. 8, 1988–Sept. 17, 1989 (cat. by Sheila Keppel, no. 3).

Literature *Catalogue of the Taft Museum,* Cincinnati, 1939 and 1958, no. 74.

1931.57

Pair of Circular Boxes with Domed Covers

Kangxi reign (Qing dynasty), ca. 1700
Porcelain, DIAM. (each) 10.8 cm (4¼ in.)
Mark: underglaze blue *lingzhi* spray within double ring

This pair of blue-and-white and famille verte circular boxes with domed covers is penciled in underglaze blue on the bases and covers with loose, composite, scrolling branches of flowering peony, lotus, chrysanthemum, and camellia within hatched-pattern borders. The finial of each box is a loop of gnarled pine glazed in aubergine and green arching over two modeled squirrels in yellow and aubergine.

The Chinese word for box and for lotus is *he,* a homophone for harmony; *he he,* as depicted on these boxes, expresses a rebus for conjugal felicity.[1] The tree squirrel is known as *song shu* (pine rodent) in Chinese and is a homophone for the pine tree, representing a wish for longevity.[2] Possibly made as a wedding gift, this pair of boxes visually expresses the wish for a long and happy marriage.

1931.57

1931.12 detail of mark

1931.12, 14

1. Wolfram Eberhard, *A Dictionary of Chinese Symbols,* trans. G. L. Campbell, London, 1991, pp. 47, 62.

2. William R. Sargent, *The Copeland Collection,* Salem, Mass., 1991, pp. 34, 67.

Provenance James A. Garland, New York (in 1895); J. Pierpont Morgan, New York (in 1904); [Parish-Watson, New York]; Taft collection, Oct. 30, 1924.

Exhibitions New York, The Metropolitan Museum of Art, *Chinese Porcelains Loaned by James A. Garland,* 1895 (cat. by John Getz, ill. opp. p. 50); Cincinnati, Taft Museum [also Flint, Mich., and Muncie, Ind.], *China in 1700: Kangxi Porcelains at the Taft Museum,* Sept. 8, 1988–Sept. 17, 1989 (cat. by Sheila Keppel, no. 69 [1931.12]).

Literature Robert Grier Cooke, *Catalogue of the Morgan Collection of Chinese Porcelains,* vol. 1, New York, 1904, nos. 104–5; *Catalogue of the Taft Museum,* Cincinnati, 1939 and 1958, nos. 459, 461.

1931.12, 1931.14

Monochromes

Baluster Vase

Kangxi reign (Qing dynasty), ca. 1700
Porcelain, H. 20.6 cm (8⅛ in.)
Mark: period underglaze blue six-character Kangxi reign mark (1662–1722)

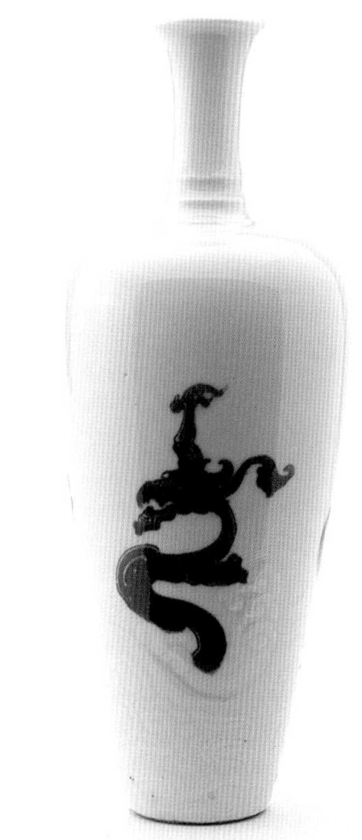

1931.135

This monochrome white slender baluster vase with ribbed trumpet neck is carved and combed in crisp relief with ribbon clouds over billowing waves in which two underglaze copper red horned *guilong,* or serpentine dragons, cavort.[1]

Although bearing a paper label that identifies this vase as number 1280 in the collection of J. Pierpont Morgan, New York, it is neither mentioned nor illustrated in the catalogue of the Morgan collection, where number 1280 is a famille rose Qianlong bottle vase decorated with peaches.[2]

1. For an identical vase, see Suzanne G. Valenstein, *A Handbook of Chinese Ceramics,* New York, 1989, p. 220, fig. 211.

2. J. Pierpont Morgan, *Catalogue of the Morgan Collection of Chinese Porcelains,* vol. II, New York, 1911, no. 1280.

1931.135 detail of mark

1931.137

Provenance [Duveen, New York]; Taft collection, Apr. 30, 1915.

Exhibition Cincinnati, Taft Museum [also Flint, Mich., and Muncie, Ind.], *China in 1700: Kangxi Porcelains at the Taft Museum,* Sept. 8, 1988–Sept. 17, 1989 (cat. by Sheila Keppel, no. 5).

Literature *Catalogue of the Taft Museum,* Cincinnati, 1939 and 1958, no. 423.

1931.135

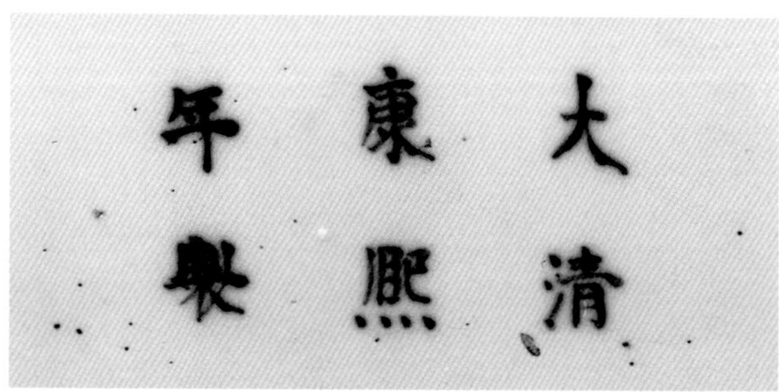

1931.137 detail of mark

Water Coupe

Kangxi reign (Qing dynasty), ca. 1705–20
Porcelain, H. 8.9 cm (3½ in.)
Mark: period underglaze blue six-character Kangxi reign mark (1662–1722)

This peach-bloom–glazed, beehive-shaped water pot has domed sides incised with three *anhua,* or secret, archaistic dragon roundels under a bright rich glaze with clouds of dusty moss green, characteristically thickening slightly at the base.

After the Kangxi emperor appointed Lang Tingji as local customs officer in 1705, the outstanding developments in new glazes such as peach bloom were made. Lang Tingji is credited with rediscovering the secret of producing copper reds—the *langyao* wares known as oxblood or sang de boeuf—which had been lost since the middle of the Ming dynasty (1368–1644).[1] The peach-bloom glaze is considered the major innovation of the Kangxi reign, and it is referred to in China by many names, including apple red, beauty's blush, baby's face, and drunken beauty.[2] Peach bloom is the Western name for the copper red glaze that the Chinese also call kidney-bean red, since it has the same red hue marked with spots of moss green as the legume.

Suzanne Valenstein writes that "the finest peachbloom wares constitute an elite series—in all likelihood consisting of no more than eight specific shapes—of small and elegant vessels that were intended to be used at the scholar's writing table. The refinement of the potting, shapes, and glaze in this group indicates that it probably dates to the final portion of the Kangxi reign."[3] The eight specific types include four types of vases or amphoras, two types of water coupes, the brush washer, and the seal color box. The Taft Museum's collection of monochromes includes seven of these eight specific shapes, lacking a bottle vase with tall cylindrical neck and applied dragon around the neck.

1. Sheila Keppel, *China in 1700: Kangxi Porcelains at the Taft Museum,* exh. cat., Cincinnati, 1988, p. 4.

2. Nigel Wood, "The Evolution of Chinese Copper Red," in *Chinese Copper-Red Wares,* ed. Rosemary E. Scott, London, 1992, p. 28.

3. Suzanne G. Valenstein, *A Handbook of Chinese Ceramics,* New York, 1989, pp. 239–40.

Provenance Startseff family, Tientsin (according to Duveen invoice); [Duveen, New York]; Taft collection, Feb. 28, 1903.

Exhibitions Cincinnati, Taft Museum, *Ming to Ch'ing: Imperial Objects and Textiles, Masterpieces of Chinese Furniture,* Feb. 12–June 30, 1975; Cincinnati, Taft Museum [also Flint, Mich., and Muncie, Ind.], *China in 1700: Kangxi Porcelains at the Taft Museum,* Sept. 8, 1988–Sept. 17, 1989 (cat. by Sheila Keppel, no. 55).

Literature John Getz, *A Catalogue of Chinese Porcelains Collected by Mr. and Mrs. Charles P. Taft,* New York, 1904, no. 37; *Catalogue of the Taft Museum,* Cincinnati, 1939 and 1958, no. 219; David Torbet Johnson, "Taft Museum," *Ventura,* vol. IV, no. 16 (June–Aug. 1991), p. 140 (ill.).

1931.137

1931.133

Water Coupe

Kangxi reign (Qing dynasty), ca. 1705–20
Porcelain, H. 8.9 cm (3½ in.)
Mark: period underglaze blue six-character Kangxi reign mark (1662–1722)

This peach-bloom–glazed, beehive-shaped water pot has domed sides incised with three *anhua,* or secret, archaistic dragon roundels under layers of the classic glaze with suspended particles of copper oxides, which result in the typical darker red dusting.

The famous Kangxi peach-bloom glaze, although essentially a pale pink-red, has many variations, including dustings of pale beige, dark red, and moss green. The mottled shadings are the result of minute copper-oxide particles, typically suspended in the center of the glaze layers to form the soft pinks, which react during the reduction firing. The larger copper particles, for example, reoxidize to green when reaching the surface of the glaze, whereas varying the concentration of copper oxide, alumina, and fluxes can result in beige dustings. Nigel Wood has recently suggested that the peach-bloom glaze was produced by a copper-lime pigment suspended between clear glazes, with the pigment probably applied by spraying.[1]

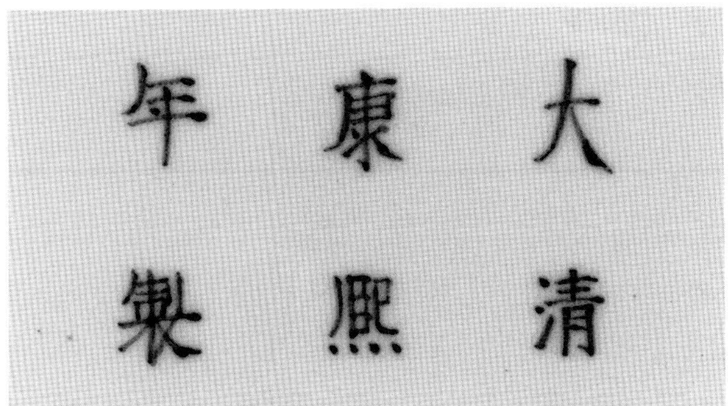

1931.133 detail of mark

1. Nigel Wood, "The Evolution of Copper Red," in *Chinese Copper-Red Wares,* ed. Rosemary E. Scott, London, 1992, p. 28.

Provenance [Thomas B. Clarke, New York]; Taft collection, Nov. 8, 1905.

Literature *Catalogue of the Taft Museum,* Cincinnati, 1939 and 1958, no. 223.

1931.133

1931.136

Brush Washer

Kangxi reign (Qing dynasty), ca. 1705–20
Porcelain, H. 5.1 cm (2 in.)
Mark: period underglaze blue six-character Kangxi reign mark (1662–1722)

This peach-bloom–glazed, shallow globular brush washer has been fired nearly to beige on one side.

Provenance [Thomas B. Clarke, New York]; Taft collection, Nov. 8, 1905.

Exhibitions Cincinnati, Taft Museum, *Ming to Ch'ing: Imperial Objects and Textiles, Masterpieces of Chinese Furniture,* Feb. 12–June 30, 1975; Cincinnati, Taft Museum [also Flint, Mich., and Muncie, Ind.], *China in*

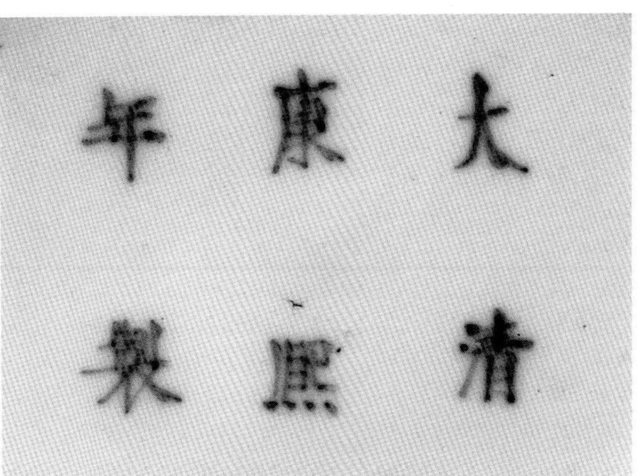

1931.136 detail of mark

1700: Kangxi Porcelains at the Taft Museum, Sept. 8, 1988–Sept. 17, 1989 (cat. by Sheila Keppel, no. 56).

Literature *Catalogue of the Taft Museum,* Cincinnati, 1939 and 1958, no. 213.

1931.136

Brush Washer

Qing dynasty, nineteenth century
Porcelain, H. 3.5 cm (1⅜ in.)
Mark: underglaze blue six-character Kangxi reign mark (1662–1722); not of the period

This peach-bloom–glazed shallow globular brush washer has patches of deep moss green dusting in the glaze.

Provenance Startseff family, Tientsin (according to Duveen invoice); [Duveen, New York]; Taft collection, Feb. 28, 1903.

Literature John Getz, *A Catalogue of Chinese Porcelains Collected by Mr. and Mrs. Charles P. Taft,* New York, 1904, no. 36; *Catalogue of the Taft Museum,* Cincinnati, 1939 and 1958, no. 209.

1931.134

1931.134

1931.134 detail of mark

1931.125

Amphora Vase

Kangxi reign (Qing dynasty), ca. 1705–20
Porcelain, H. 20.3 cm (8 in.)
Mark: period underglaze blue six-character Kangxi reign mark (1662–1722)

This peach-bloom–glazed amphora vase has a slender baluster body with two horizontal ribs at the base of the short slender trumpet neck. The creamy glaze is a rich deep color.

Provenance Puyi, who reigned as a boy under the title Xuantong, 1909–11 (according to Parish-Watson invoice); [Parish-Watson, New York]; Taft collection, Dec. 22, 1924.

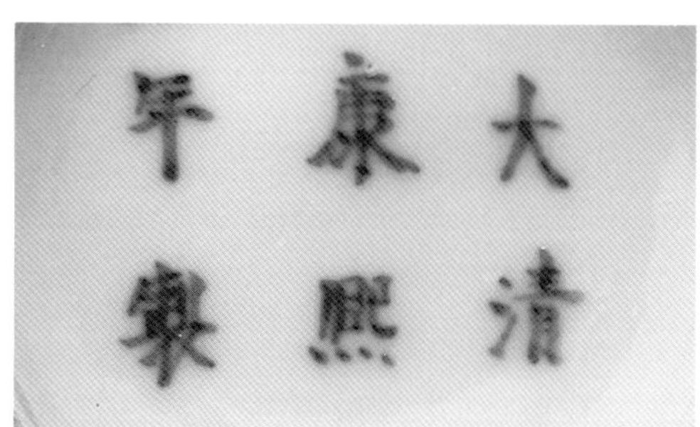

1931.125 detail of mark

Exhibition Cincinnati, Taft Museum [also Flint, Mich., and Muncie, Ind.], *China in 1700: Kangxi Porcelains at the Taft Museum,* Sept. 8, 1988–Sept. 17, 1989 (cat. by Sheila Keppel, no. 13).

Literature *Catalogue of the Taft Museum,* Cincinnati, 1939 and 1958, no. 216.

1931.125

Amphora Vase

Kangxi reign (Qing dynasty), ca. 1705–20
Porcelain, H. 15.2 cm (6 in.)
Mark erased

This small peach-bloom–glazed amphora has a slender body tapering from sloping shoulders below a delicate trumpet neck. The classic rich glaze has clouds of pale beige and moss green.

The lip and base have been ground down.

Provenance [Thomas B. Clarke, New York]; Taft collection, Nov. 8, 1905.

Exhibition Cincinnati, Taft Museum [also Flint, Mich., and Muncie, Ind.], *China in 1700: Kangxi Porcelains at the Taft Museum,* Sept. 8, 1988–Sept. 17, 1989 (cat. by Sheila Keppel, no. 57).

Literature *Catalogue of the Taft Museum,* Cincinnati, 1939 and 1958, no. 214.

1931.127

1931.127

Amphora Vase

Qing dynasty, nineteenth century
Porcelain, H. 15.8 cm (6¼ in.)
Mark: underglaze blue six-character Kangxi reign mark (1662–1722); not of the period

This small peach-bloom–glazed amphora has a slender body tapering from sloping shoulders below a delicate trumpet neck. The peach-bloom glaze is of a light, almost ashes-of-roses, color.

1931.123

1931.123 detail of mark

The period amphoras normally have tall, unglazed, hollow bases that have sometimes been ground or cut down. In the case of this example, the base is as it was originally intended.

Provenance Mrs. Potter Palmer, Paris (according to Parish-Watson invoice); [Parish-Watson, New York]; Taft collection, Apr. 14, 1924.

Literature *Catalogue of the Taft Museum,* Cincinnati, 1939 and 1958, no. 218.

1931.123

Bottle Vase

Kangxi reign (Qing dynasty), ca. 1705–20
Porcelain, H. 20.6 cm (8⅛ in.)
Mark: period underglaze blue six-character Kangxi reign mark (1662–1722)

This peach-bloom–glazed bottle vase has a slender body molded with a band of petals at the base. It is covered in a mottled glaze of pale moss green and peach bloom.

The lip has been ground down.

1931.132 detail of mark

Provenance Robert Hoe, Mendelssohn Hall, New York (sale, American Art Galleries, New York, Feb. 16, 1911, no. 387?); Frederick William Hunter, New York (sale, American Art Galleries, New York, Jan. 7–10, 12–14, 1920, no. 689 [ill.]); [Parish-Watson, New York]; Taft collection, Apr. 14, 1924.

Literature *Catalogue of the Taft Museum,* Cincinnati, 1939 and 1958, no. 227.

1931.132

Oviform Vase

Qing dynasty, nineteenth century
Porcelain, H. 20.9 cm (8¼ in.)
Mark: underglaze blue six-character Kangxi reign mark (1662–1722); not of the period

1931.132

1931.128

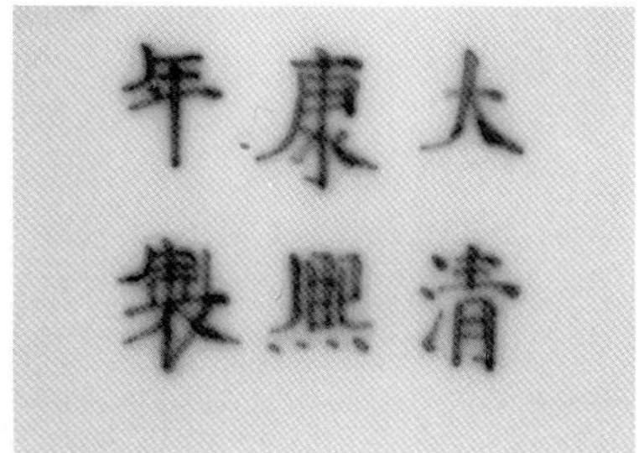

1931.128 detail of mark

This peach-bloom–glazed slender oviform vase with a tall trumpet neck is carved above the thickening foot ring with a row of chrysanthemum petals.

Although this bottle vase is of the same shape as the preceding example, it was produced at a different kiln. A likely explanation is that it is a nineteenth-century forgery, falsely marked with the *nianhao* of the Kangxi emperor. The increase in Western demand for genuine eighteenth-century peach blooms led to spurious marks on nineteenth-century copies. The Chinese veneration of highly prized ceramics such as peach blooms produced during earlier periods is another possible reason for the production of forgeries. Recently, however, Anthony du Boulay has suggested that at certain times nonimperial kilns assisted with the production of official court orders. In that case, the Taft vase, in fact, could be of the Kangxi period.[1]

1. Letter to David Torbet Johnson from Anthony du Boulay, July 6, 1992.

Provenance Richard Bennett, Thornby Hall, Northampton (sale, Christie's, London, n.d., no. 357?); [Gorer, London]; [Parish-Watson, New York]; Taft collection, Nov. 9, 1923.

Literature Edgar Gorer and J. F. Blacker, *Chinese Porcelains and Hard Stones,* vol. II, London, 1911, pl. 60; *Catalogue of the Taft Museum,* Cincinnati, 1939 and 1958, no. 225.

1931.128

Boxes with Domed Covers

Qing dynasty, nineteenth century
Porcelain, H. 3.8 cm (1½ in.)
Mark: underglaze blue six-character Kangxi reign mark (1662–1722); not of the period

These four peach-bloom–glazed circular boxes with domed covers held seal ink. The classic glazes have been variously fired from mottled gray-pink to pale moss green.

1931.129, 124, 126, 131

1931.129, 124, 126, 131 detail of marks

Provenance 1931.131, James W. Ellsworth (sale, Anderson Galleries, New York, Apr. 27–28, 30, May 1, 1923); [Parish-Watson, New York]; Taft collection, Apr. 14, 1924. 1931.124, 126, 129 [Thomas B. Clarke, New York]; Taft collection, Nov. 8, 1905.

Exhibition Cincinnati, Taft Museum, *Ming to Ch'ing: Imperial Objects and Textiles, Masterpieces of Chinese Furniture,* Feb. 12–June 30, 1975 (one of the four).

Literature *Catalogue of the Taft Museum,* Cincinnati, 1939 and 1958, nos. 220, 222, 224, 228.

1931.124, 1931.126, 1931.129, 1931.131

Bottle Vase

Kangxi reign (Qing dynasty), ca. 1705–20
Porcelain, H. 39.4 cm (15½ in.)
Unmarked

This globular bottle vase with a tall slender neck is covered with a finely crackled clear copper red glaze called *langyao,* or oxblood (also known as sang de boeuf), over a white slip. The glaze thickens toward the ground foot ring.

During the fifteenth century in the Ming dynasty (1368–1644), this copper red glaze was known as fresh red or sacrificial red. The four sacrificial colors are red, for the earth; blue, for the heavens; yellow, for the emperor; and white, for the dead. It is extremely difficult to distinguish early-fifteenth-century copper red glazes from those produced during the early Qing dynasty, even though the chemical compositions of the two related glazes are different.[1] Qing dynasty copper red glazes are richer in calcia, higher in alumina, and lower in silica and alkalis.[2] One of the important innovations of the Kangxi period, along with the peach-bloom glaze, the particular shade of this bottle vase has been likened to that of a ripe cherry.

1. Nigel Wood, "The Evolution of Chinese Copper Red," in *Chinese Copper-Red Wares,* ed. Rosemary E. Scott, London, 1992, p. 27.
2. Letter to David Torbet Johnson from Anthony du Boulay, July 6, 1992.

Provenance James A. Garland, New York (sale, American Art Galleries, New York, Jan. 17, 1924, no. 81 [ill.], for $8,300); [Parish-Watson, New York]; Taft collection, Dec. 22, 1924.

Exhibition Cincinnati, Taft Museum [also Flint, Mich., and Muncie, Ind.], *China in 1700: Kangxi Porcelains at the Taft Museum,* Sept. 8, 1988–Sept. 17, 1989 (cat. by Sheila Keppel, no. 6).

Literature *Catalogue of the Taft Museum,* Cincinnati, 1939 and 1958, no. 202 (ill.).

1931.105

1931.105

1931.107

Bottle Vase

Kangxi reign (Qing dynasty), ca. 1705–20
Porcelain, H. 40.6 cm (16 in.)
Unmarked

This globular bottle vase with a tall slender neck is covered with an irregular and closely crackled, clear, copper red glaze called *langyao,* or oxblood (also known as sang de boeuf), over a dribbled white slip. The glaze pools at the ground foot ring.

Provenance Startseff family, Tientsin (according to Duveen invoice); [Duveen, New York]; Taft collection, Feb. 28, 1903.

Literature John Getz, *A Catalogue of Chinese Porcelains Collected by Mr. and Mrs. Charles P. Taft,* New York, 1904, no. 35; *Catalogue of the Taft Museum,* Cincinnati, 1939 and 1958, no. 201.

1931.107

Vase

Kangxi reign (Qing dynasty), ca. 1705–20
Porcelain, H. 11.7 cm (4⅝ in.)
Unmarked

This small vase with a compressed pear-shaped body stands on a short narrow base and has a tall slender neck. It is covered in an irregularly crackled and mottled copper red glaze called *langyao,* or oxblood (also known as sang de boeuf).

Provenance [Thomas B. Clarke, New York]; Taft collection, Nov. 8, 1905.

Exhibition Cincinnati, Taft Museum [also Flint, Mich., and Muncie, Ind.], *China in 1700: Kangxi Porcelains at the Taft Museum,* Sept. 8, 1988–Sept. 17, 1989 (cat. by Sheila Keppel, no. 7).

Literature *Catalogue of the Taft Museum,* Cincinnati, 1939 and 1958, no. 431.

1931.103

Vase

Qianlong reign (Qing dynasty), ca. 1736–95
Porcelain, H. 10.8 cm (4¼ in.)
Unmarked

This small vase with a slightly compressed pear-shaped body stands on a high narrow foot ring and has a slender trumpet neck. It is covered in a crackled and mottled copper red glaze called *langyao,* or oxblood (also known as sang de boeuf).

Later in the eighteenth century, following the end of the reign of the Kangxi emperor in 1722, the production of *langyao* glazes continued, but with more irregularity in control, particularly around the foot ring, as on this example. The mottled appearance of the glaze on the body of this vase is another indication that it was more likely made during the Qianlong period than the Kangxi reign.[1] See the preceding vase for an example from about 1705–20.

1. Letter to David Torbet Johnson from Anthony du Boulay, Aug. 1, 1992.

1931.103

1931.101

Provenance James W. Ellsworth, New York; [Parish-Watson, New York]; Taft collection, Apr. 14, 1924.

Literature *Catalogue of the Taft Museum,* Cincinnati, 1939 and 1958, no. 433.

1931.101

Bottle Vase

Qianlong reign (Qing dynasty), ca. 1750–95
Porcelain, H. 27.9 cm (11 in.)
Unmarked

This monochrome bottle vase with broad oviform body and cylindrical neck, its classic proportions finely potted, is covered in a matte soufflé ashes-of-roses copper-oxide glaze.

Provenance Henry Sampson, New York; [Parish-Watson, New York]; Taft collection, Feb. 17, 1928.

Exhibition Cincinnati, Taft Museum [also Flint, Mich., and Muncie, Ind.], *China in 1700: Kangxi Porcelains at the Taft Museum,* Sept. 8, 1988–Sept. 17, 1989 (cat. by Sheila Keppel, no. 9).

Literature *Catalogue of the Taft Museum,* Cincinnati, 1939 and 1958, no. 430.

1931.117

1931.117

1931.186

Bottle Vase

Qianlong reign (Qing Dynasty), ca. 1735–40
Porcelain, H. 34.3 cm (13½ in.)
Unmarked

This monochrome pink pear-shaped bottle vase has a bulb mouth above raised double rings on the neck and is covered with a soufflé rose pink enamel, derived from a precipitate of gold chloride rather than the usual copper oxide.

Provenance [Duveen, New York]; Taft collection, Nov. 10, 1905.

Literature *Catalogue of the Taft Museum,* Cincinnati, 1939 and 1958, no. 508.

1931.186

Bottle Vase

Kangxi reign (Qing dynasty), ca. 1705–20
Porcelain, H. 31.7 cm (12½ in.)
Unmarked

This monochrome bottle vase with globular body and cylindrical neck is glazed in pale copper red and dressed in a clear apple

1931.113

green with iridescent flakes and faint traces of gilt decoration remaining.

During the early twentieth century, when collections of monochromes, especially peach blooms and apple greens, were highly prized, the gilding on this vase was removed by abrasion, and the surface was then lightly wheel-polished in an attempt to regain the high gloss of the original glaze. The combination of complementary colors such as red and green, which symbolize life, as seen on this example, is highly regarded by the Chinese.

Provenance Henry Sampson, New York; [Parish-Watson, New York]; Taft collection, Feb. 17, 1928.

Literature *Catalogue of the Taft Museum,* Cincinnati, 1939 and 1958, no. 438.

1931.113

Meiping

Qing dynasty, early eighteenth century
Porcelain, H. 17.8 cm (7 in.)
Unmarked

This apple green–glazed *meiping* has the classic slender baluster body and short, slightly everted neck. It is covered with an irregularly crackled high-fired bluish glaze under a translucent green enamel, known as *pingguoqing* in Chinese, and a clear overglaze.

The lip has been ground down.

Provenance [Thomas B. Clarke, New York]; Taft collection, Nov. 8, 1905.

Exhibition Cincinnati, Taft Museum [also Flint, Mich., and Muncie, Ind.], *China in 1700: Kangxi Porcelains at the Taft Museum,* Sept. 8, 1988–Sept. 17, 1989 (cat. by Sheila Keppel, no. 15).

Literature *Catalogue of the Taft Museum,* Cincinnati, 1939 and 1958, no. 332.

1931.104

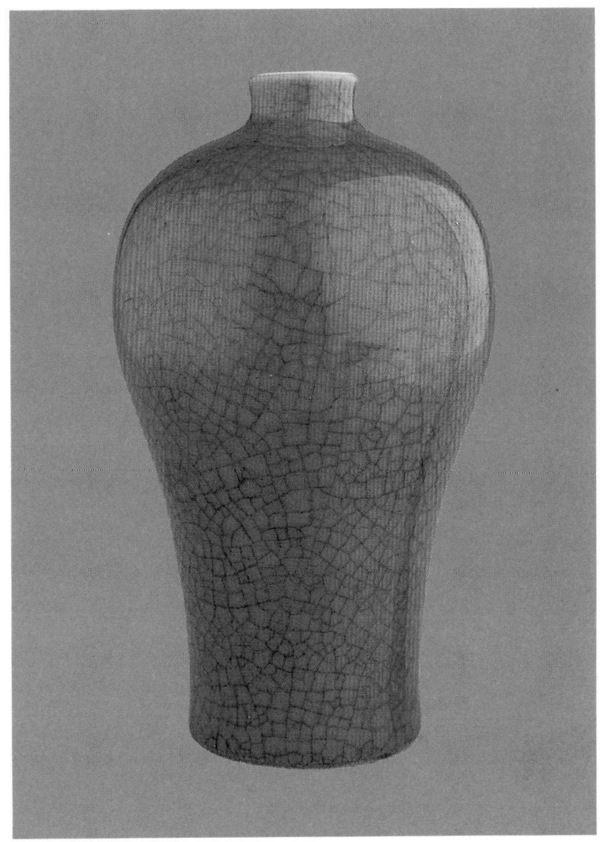

1931.104

Meiping

Kangxi reign (Qing dynasty), ca. 1700–1722
Porcelain, H. 18.1 cm (7⅛ in.)
Unmarked

This apple green–glazed *meiping* has the classic slender baluster body and short, slightly everted neck. It is covered with an irregularly crackled high-fired bluish glaze under a translucent green enamel and a subtly opalescent clear overglaze.

The lip has been ground down.

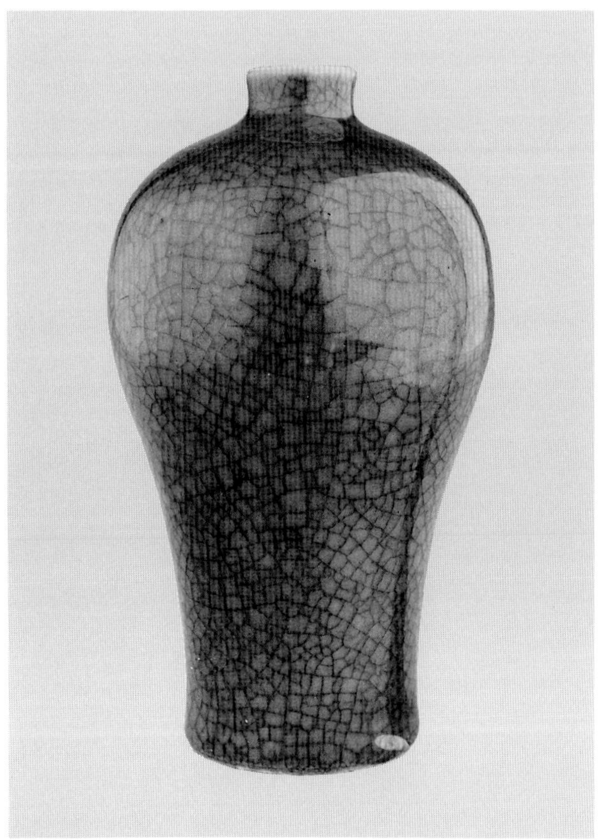

1931.100

Provenance General Brayton Ives; Charles D. Barney; [Parish-Watson, New York]; Taft collection, Apr. 14, 1924.

Literature *Catalogue of the Taft Museum,* Cincinnati, 1939 and 1958, no. 327.

1931.100

Oviform Vase

Qing dynasty, eighteenth century
Porcelain, H. 14.6 cm (5¾ in.)
Unmarked

This apple green–glazed oviform vase with short everted neck is covered with a thick crackled bluish glaze dressed with an opalescent bright green enamel.

Provenance Startseff family, Tientsin (according to Duveen invoice); [Duveen, New York (as early Kangxi)]; Taft collection, Feb. 28, 1903.

Literature John Getz, *A Catalogue of Chinese Porcelains Collected by Mr. and Mrs. Charles P. Taft,* New York, 1904, no. 34; *Catalogue of the Taft Museum,* Cincinnati, 1939 and 1958, no. 427.

1931.102

1931.102

Bottle Vase

Qing dynasty, ca. 1800–1850
Porcelain, H. 21.9 cm (8⅝ in.)
Unmarked

1931.110

This bottle vase, with a pear-shaped body and tall cylindrical neck, is covered with a bright leaf green glaze. An attendant punting toward two gentlemen conversing below trees on an outcrop of rockwork is painted in blue underglaze that looks black.

Provenance [Duveen, New York (as Yongzheng)]; Taft collection, Nov. 5, 1903.

Literature John Getz, *A Catalogue of Chinese Porcelains Collected by Mr. and Mrs. Charles P. Taft,* New York, 1904, no. 3; *Catalogue of the Taft Museum,* Cincinnati, 1939 and 1958, no. 293.

1931.110

Oviform Jar with Domed Cover

Qing dynasty, late eighteenth–early nineteenth century
Porcelain, H. 25.1 cm (9⅞ in.)
Unmarked

This oviform jar with domed cover is covered in a crackled bluish white glaze, which is dressed in a brilliant clear apple green with iridescent flakes in the crackle.

This *craquelure,* one among many variants, was carefully induced by slowing or accelerating the cooling process after firing. The cover, probably originally from a larger storage jar, is contemporary to this jar but was married to it later.

Provenance Prince Kung Pu Wei (sale, Christie's, London, 1913); [Parish-Watson, New York (as Kangxi, "with original dome cover")]; Taft collection, Dec. 22, 1924.

Exhibition Cincinnati, Taft Museum [also Flint, Mich., and Muncie, Ind.], *China in 1700: Kangxi Porcelains at the Taft Museum,* Sept. 8, 1988–Sept. 17, 1989 (cat. by Sheila Keppel, no. 19).

Literature *Catalogue of the Taft Museum,* Cincinnati, 1939 and 1958, no. 432.

1931.106

1931.106

1989.2

Pair of Melon-shaped Vases

Qing dynasty, ca. 1900
Porcelain, H. 14 cm (5½ in.)
Unmarked

This pair of slender melon-shaped vases has carved vertical segment flutes. Both are covered with crackled, dark leaf green glaze.

Provenance [Duveen, New York]; Taft collection, Nov. 10, 1905.

1989.2–3

Beaker Vase

Qianlong reign (Qing dynasty), ca. 1750–95
Porcelain, H. 29.2 cm (11½ in.)
Mark: period impressed underglaze six-character Qianlong reign seal (1736–95)

The form of this monochrome slender trumpet-shaped vase is taken from a Shang dynasty (ca. 1600–ca. 1030 B.C.) bronze *gu* beaker. The bulbous central section is incised with loose *taotie,* or a highly stylized face or top jaw of a dragon, between long overlapping leaf motifs and bands of key pattern on the base and neck. The vase is covered in a closely crackled brilliant clear kingfisher blue glaze.

1931.115

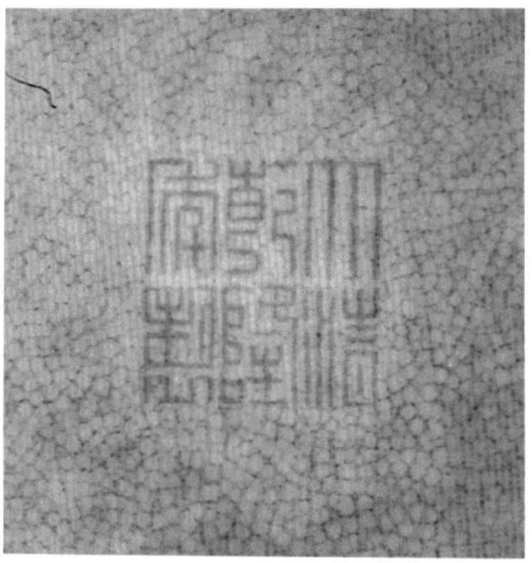

1931.115 detail of mark

The kingfisher blue glaze, made from copper fluxed with potash, first appeared in the fourteenth century. When opacified with arsenic during the second quarter of the eighteenth century it became a very popular new glaze (see the following entry as an example).

Subtle but interesting differences can be noted when comparing this vase to two similar but unmarked vases in the Percival David Foundation (London), which have the same decoration but are molded rather than incised (inv. nos. B588, 589).[1]

1. Rosemary E. Scott, *Elegant Form and Harmonious Decoration: Four Dynasties of Jingdezhen Porcelain*, London, 1992, p. 153, fig. 176.

Provenance [Duveen, New York (as Kangxi)]; Taft collection, Nov. 10, 1905.

Exhibition Cincinnati, Taft Museum [also Flint, Mich., and Muncie, Ind.], *China in 1700: Kangxi Porcelains at the Taft Museum*, Sept. 8, 1988–Sept. 17, 1989 (cat. by Sheila Keppel, no. 16).

Literature *Catalogue of the Taft Museum*, Cincinnati, 1939 and 1958, no. 434.

1931.115

Bowl

Late Qianlong reign (Qing dynasty), ca. 1790
Porcelain, H. 16.5 x DIAM. 21 cm (6½ x 8¼ in.)
Unmarked

This deep bowl is decorated with the impressed rice-grain motif. Formal flowers outlined in black decorate a pale turquoise, or *jicui*, ground between bands of dotted lappets and flowered *ruyi* heads in gilt on underglaze blue grounds.

Although the technique used to decorate this bowl is known as impressed rice-grain, the kernel-shaped holes in the walls of the vessel were cut by a skilled artisan using a small flexible knife while the clay was still soft. A clear glaze was then added to coat the pierced design, resulting in the holes being filled with translucent pools of glaze.

The form of this deep bowl with inverted lip resembles that of the ancient Buddhistic begging bowl.

Provenance [Duveen, New York (as Yongzheng)]; Taft collection, Mar. 28, 1908.

1931.165

Exhibition Cincinnati, Taft Museum [also Flint, Mich., and Muncie, Ind.], *China in 1700: Kangxi Porcelains at the Taft Museum,* Sept. 8, 1988–Sept. 17, 1989 (cat. by Sheila Keppel, no. 11).

Literature *Catalogue of the Taft Museum,* Cincinnati, 1939 and 1958, no. 204 (ill.).

1931.165

Bottle-Gourd Vase

Kangxi reign (Qing dynasty), ca. 1700
Porcelain, H. 11.7 cm (4⅝ in.)
Unmarked

This small monochrome double gourd–shaped bottle vase is covered in a thick, opaque, mirror-black glaze.

The brilliant deep effect of this mirrorlike surface was achieved by multiple coats of the *wujin,* or "black bronze," glaze, containing a combination of iron and manganese oxides with the addition of small amounts of cobalt and copper.

The bottle gourd, called *hulu* in Chinese, or calabash in the West (*Lagenaria siceraria*), has numerous associations in China, including purity, longevity, and fecundity. As Terese Tse Bartholomew explains, the bottle gourd is used as a vessel to store food, liquor, and medicine, thus representing abundance and good luck. Since the bottle gourd produces so many seeds, it is also a symbol of fertility.[1] In addition, Daoist Immortals use it as a weapon when threatened by opposing forces (see 1931.146, pp. 642–43, and 1931.160, p. 644): clouds of blackbirds or fierce rainstorms are released from the vessels to frighten enemies during battles, or the bottle gourd is uncorked to absorb the evil vapors of the universe. The shape of the bottle gourd symbolizes a union of heaven and earth as well.[2]

1. Terese Tse Bartholomew, *The Hundred Flowers: Botanical Motifs in Chinese Art,* exh. cat., Asian Art Museum of San Francisco, 1985, no. 35.
2. Wolfram Eberhard, *A Dictionary of Chinese Symbols,* trans. G. L. Campbell, London, 1991, p. 46.

Provenance [Thomas B. Clarke, New York]; Taft collection, Nov. 8, 1905.

Exhibition Cincinnati, Taft Museum [also Flint, Mich., and Muncie, Ind.], *China in 1700: Kangxi Porcelains at the Taft Museum,* Sept. 8, 1988–Sept. 17, 1989 (cat. by Sheila Keppel, no. 14).

Literature *Catalogue of the Taft Museum,* Cincinnati, 1939 and 1958, no. 357.

1931.98

Oviform Vase

Kangxi reign (Qing dynasty), ca. 1700–1722
Porcelain, H. 21.6 cm (8½ in.)
Unmarked

This celadon-glazed slender oviform vase with a short trumpet neck is carved and engraved on the body under the glaze with two spirited horned bird-dragons cavorting among breaking waves under a clear pale glaze.

1931.98

1931.130

The celadons of the Kangxi period were produced by firing a glaze containing traces of iron oxide and other minerals in a reducing atmosphere.

Provenance [Thomas B. Clarke, New York]; Taft collection, Nov. 8, 1905.

Exhibitions Cincinnati, Taft Museum, *Ming to Ch'ing: Imperial Objects and Textiles, Masterpieces of Chinese Furniture,* Feb. 12–June 30, 1975; Cincinnati, Taft Museum [also Flint, Mich., and Muncie, Ind.], *China in 1700: Kangxi Porcelains at the Taft Museum,* Sept. 8, 1988–Sept. 17, 1989 (cat. by Sheila Keppel, no. 12).

Literature *Catalogue of the Taft Museum,* Cincinnati, 1939 and 1958, no. 221.

1931.130

1989.1 detail of mark

Pear-shaped Vase

Qianlong reign (Qing dynasty), ca. 1760–95
Porcelain, H. 27.5 cm (10¾ in.)
Mark: period impressed underglaze blue six-character Qianlong reign seal (1736–95)

This celadon-glazed pear-shaped vase stands on a short foot ring with openwork leafy handles set on the trumpet neck below the everted lip. The whole vase is carved with overlapping peony petals and covered in a faintly crackled celadon glaze.

1989.1

1989.1

Brush Washer

Kangxi reign (Qing dynasty), ca. 1700–1722
Porcelain, H. 4.5 x DIAM. 11.5 cm (1¾ x 4½ in.)
Mark: period underglaze blue six-character Kangxi reign mark (1662–1722)

This clair-de-lune–glazed shallow globular brush washer with a wide delicate foot ring has been ground down on the inside lip.

Yuebai, or "moon blue," was produced with a subtle glaze of the palest cobalt oxide. According to Suzanne Valenstein, "*Clair de lune*–glazed porcelains frequently have the same shapes as the classic peachbloom vessels, and like the latter, show the daintiness and fineness of potting that is associated with the end of the Kangxi period."[1]

1931.118

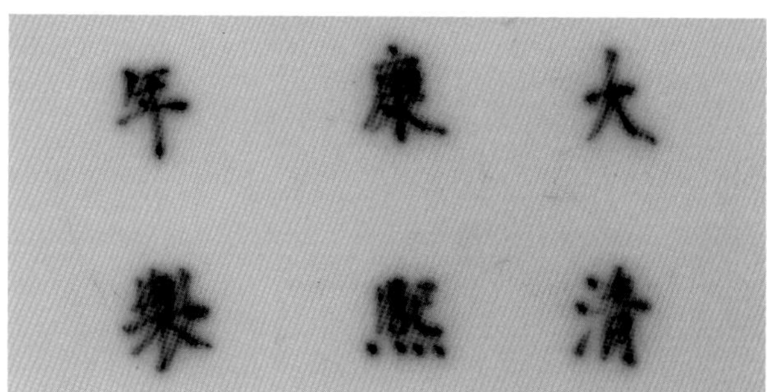

1931.118 detail of mark

1. Suzanne G. Valenstein, *A Handbook of Chinese Ceramics*, New York, 1989, p. 241.

Provenance James W. Ellsworth; [Parish-Watson, New York]; Taft collection, Apr. 14, 1924.

Exhibition Cincinnati, Taft Museum [also Flint, Mich., and Muncie, Ind.], *China in 1700: Kangxi Porcelains at the Taft Museum*, Sept. 8, 1988–Sept. 17, 1989 (cat. by Sheila Keppel, no. 10).

Literature *Catalogue of the Taft Museum*, Cincinnati, 1939 and 1958, no. 215.

1931.118

Brush Washer

Qing dynasty, nineteenth century
Porcelain, H. (without lid) 4.4 x DIAM. 12.7 cm ($1\frac{3}{4}$ x 5 in.)
Mark: underglaze blue six-character Kangxi reign mark (1662–1722); not of the period

This clair-de-lune–glazed shallow globular brush washer with wide delicate foot ring is somewhat heavily potted but similar to the preceding example.

Provenance [Thomas B. Clarke, New York]; Taft collection, Nov. 8, 1905.

Exhibition Cincinnati, Taft Museum, *Ming to Ch'ing: Imperial Objects and Textiles, Masterpieces of Chinese Furniture*, Feb. 12–June 30, 1975.

Literature *Catalogue of the Taft Museum*, Cincinnati, 1939 and 1958, no. 217.

1931.122

1931.122

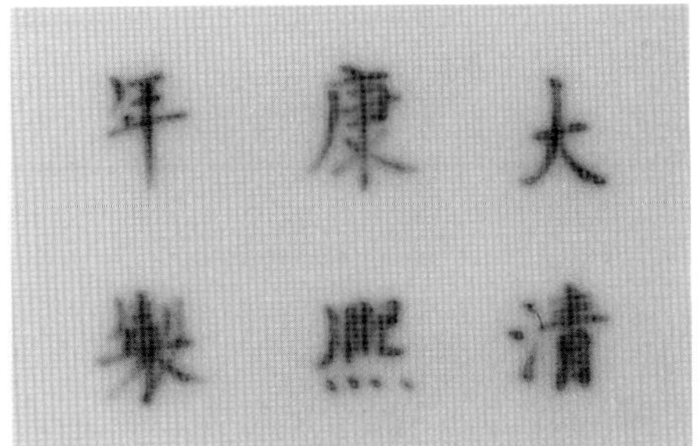

1931.122 detail of mark

1931.120

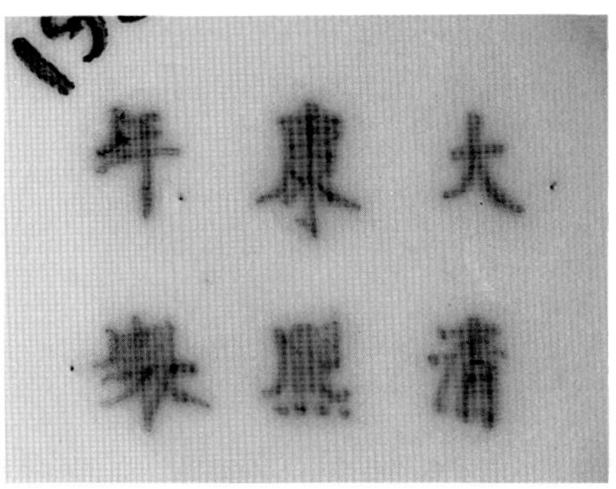

1931.120 detail of mark

Water Coupe

Qing dynasty, nineteenth century
Porcelain, H. 7.3 cm ($2\frac{7}{8}$ in.)
Mark: underglaze blue six-character Kangxi reign mark (1662–1722); not of the period

This clair-de-lune–glazed water pot has a globular body with a short everted neck recessed into the shoulder. The glaze is an even pale blue.

The form of this coupe is one of the eight prescribed shapes for peach blooms, which is not otherwise represented in the Taft collection (see 1931.137, p. 596).

Provenance [Parish-Watson, New York]; Taft collection, Apr. 14, 1924.

Literature *Catalogue of the Taft Museum*, Cincinnati, 1939 and 1958, no. 211.

1931.120

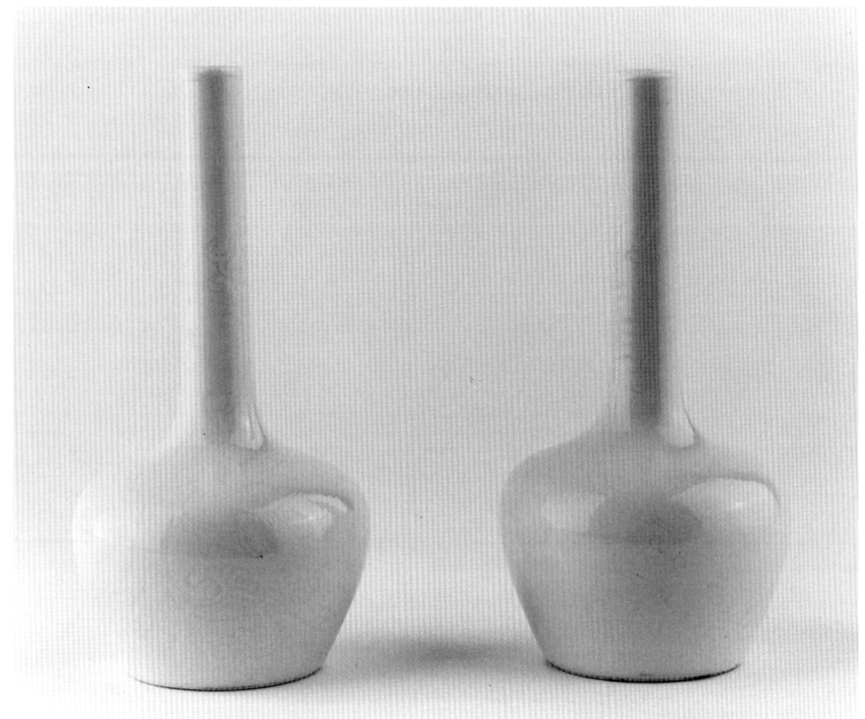

1931.119, 121

1931.119 detail of mark

Pair of Bottles

Yongzheng reign (Qing dynasty), ca. 1730
Porcelain, H. 11.8 cm ($4\frac{5}{8}$ in.)
Mark: period underglaze blue six-character Yongzheng reign mark (1723–35)

These two small monochrome white bottles with short tapering globular bodies and tall cylindrical necks are each decorated under a pale blue-white glaze with *anhua,* or secret, incised dragons and foliage on the body and flowers on the neck.

Provenance 1931.119, William N. Pethick, China (according to Clarke invoice); 1931.121, imperial household (according to Clarke invoice); [both, Thomas B. Clarke, New York]; Taft collection, Nov. 8, 1905.

Exhibition Cincinnati, Taft Museum [also Flint, Mich., and Muncie, Ind.], *China in 1700: Kangxi Porcelains at the Taft Museum,* Sept. 8, 1988–Sept. 17, 1989 (cat. by Sheila Keppel, no. 17 [1931.119]).

Literature *Catalogue of the Taft Museum,* Cincinnati, 1939 and 1958, nos. 210, 212.

1931.119, 1931.121

Bottle

Yongzheng reign (Qing dynasty), 1723–35
Porcelain, H. 18.4 cm ($7\frac{1}{4}$ in.)
Mark: period impressed underglaze six-character Yongzheng reign seal (1723–35)

1931.112

This monochrome white bottle has a flattened globular body incised with the *babao,* or Eight Precious Things, tied with long ribbons between crisply molded and engraved overlapping *lingzhi* fungus. The tall slender neck is horizontally ribbed below a flaring lip.

1931.112 detail of mark

Provenance [Thomas B. Clarke, New York]; Taft collection, Nov. 8, 1905.

Exhibition Cincinnati, Taft Museum [also Flint, Mich., and Muncie, Ind.], *China in 1700: Kangxi Porcelains at the Taft Museum,* Sept. 8, 1988–Sept. 17, 1989 (cat. by Sheila Keppel, no. 20).

Literature *Catalogue of the Taft Museum,* Cincinnati, 1939 and 1958, no. 441.

1931.112

Hexafoil Oviform Vase

Jiaqing reign (Qing dynasty), ca. 1800–1810
Porcelain, H. 22.9 cm (9 in.)
Mark: period impressed underglaze six-character Jiaqing reign seal (1796–1820)

This monochrome white hexafoil oviform vase is molded in crisp relief with loose stylized branches of flowering peony above a band of ribbed false lappets. The petal-shaped lip of the flaring neck is turned out and molded with bats. The vase is covered with a widely crackled brilliant white glaze.

Bats, or *fu* in Chinese, are a popular rebus subject since the word for "blessing" shares the same sound. Typically shown upside down, or *dao,* which is homophonous for "arrived," the upside-down bats on the lip of this vase form a pun meaning "happiness has arrived."[1]

1931.108

1. Terese Tse Bartholomew, *Myths and Rebuses in Chinese Art,* exh. cat., Asian Art Museum of San Francisco, 1988, n.p.

Provenance [Duveen, New York (as Yongzheng)]; Taft collection, Nov. 5, 1903.

Literature John Getz, *A Catalogue of Chinese Porcelains Collected by Mr. and Mrs. Charles P. Taft,* New York, 1904, no. 30; *Catalogue of the Taft Museum,* Cincinnati, 1939 and 1958, no. 439.

1931.108

1931.108 detail of mark

Oviform Vase

Qing dynasty, ca. 1820
Porcelain, H. 10.5 cm (4⅛ in.)
Unmarked

This small monochrome oviform vase with short everted neck is covered in a clear yellow glaze over a thick crackled white slip.

1931.96

Provenance Henry Sampson, New York; [Parish-Watson, New York (as Kangxi and "unique monochrome")]; Taft collection, Apr. 14, 1924.

Exhibition Cincinnati, Taft Museum [also Flint, Mich., and Muncie, Ind.], *China in 1700: Kangxi Porcelains at the Taft Museum,* Sept. 8, 1988–Sept. 17, 1989 (cat. by Sheila Keppel, no. 18).

Literature *Catalogue of the Taft Museum,* Cincinnati, 1939 and 1958, no. 359.

1931.96

Bottle Vase

Daoguang reign (Qing dynasty), ca. 1821–50
Porcelain, H. 16.5 cm (6½ in.)
Mark: period impressed underglaze aubergine six-character Daoguang reign seal (1821–50)

This small bottle vase with oviform body and cylindrical neck is covered in a minutely crackled clear egg-yolk yellow glaze.

1931.218

1931.218 detail of mark

Provenance Startseff family, Tientsin (according to Clarke invoice); [Thomas B. Clarke, New York]; Taft collection, Nov. 8, 1905.

Exhibition Cincinnati, Taft Museum [also Flint, Mich., and Muncie, Ind.], *China in 1700: Kangxi Porcelains at the Taft Museum,* Sept. 8, 1988–Sept. 17, 1989 (cat. by Sheila Keppel, no. 8).

Literature *Catalogue of the Taft Museum,* Cincinnati, 1939 and 1958, no. 429.

1931.218

Brush Washer

Qing dynasty, Guangdong province, late eighteenth or early nineteenth century
Stoneware, H. 8.2 cm (3¼ in.)
Unmarked

This lotus-bud brush washer has a heavy stoneware body modeled in relief with a *guilong,* or serpentine dragon, clambering over the side. It is covered with a widely crackled creamy bright blue glaze of the *jun* type.

Provenance Taft collection, after 1904.

Literature *Catalogue of the Taft Museum,* Cincinnati, 1939 and 1958, no. 425.

1931.228

1931.228

Famille Verte

Famille verte is a term coined by the French scholar-collector Albert Jacquemart during the mid-nineteenth century and disseminated into the international ceramics vocabulary through his 1862 publication, *Histoire artistique, industrielle et commerciale de la porcelaine*, which Jacquemart coauthored with E. le Blant. Called *yingcai*, or "bright colors," in Chinese, famille verte porcelains are easily distinguishable by the predominance of brilliant copper green. Developed from the Ming dynasty *wucai*, or "five-color," wares, but differing by the replacement of turquoise blue with aubergine or purplish blue, famille verte enamels reached a zenith of production under Cang Yingxuan, who was appointed director of the Jingdezhen factory in 1683. The famille jaune (with yellow predominating) and famille noire (with black predominating) palettes were developed from the low-fired famille verte palette of translucent, lead-silicate enamels.

Guandi, Daoist God of War

Kangxi reign (Qing dynasty), ca. 1700
Porcelain and hair, H. 26.6 cm (10½ in.)
Unmarked

This famille verte figure of Guandi, the Daoist god of war, is seated, right hand raised, at ease on a brocade-draped flowered stool. He wears a belted dragon robe over relief-molded studded breastplate and leg armor, masked boots, and an official's ribboned headdress and diadem. The figure is enameled on the biscuit in green, aubergine, yellow, turquoise, and blue and outlined in black with dragons above waves and scattered flowers. Long strands of hair — which are apparently either human or horse hair — are plugged into his chin, under his nose as mustaches, and below his ears. The back is painted with a sketchy landscape in black.

Guandi (or Emperor Guan) is the name given to the Daoist god of war and justice, created around 1600 from the historical figure Guan Yu, a general of the Minor Han (Shuhan) dynasty established in Sichuan during the Three Kingdoms (A.D. 220–65). Guan Yu, the hero of the epic tale *Sanguozhi Yanyi (The Romance of the Three Kingdoms)*, made a pact with Liu Bei, a member of the Han dynasty royal family, and Chang Fei, a butcher, to reunite their country around A.D. 200. Guan Yu, also known as Guan Gong, died during his attempts (in the novel he is described as "joining the gods"), and the country remained divided after his death.[1] As an important historical person, hero, and scholar, Guandi is often appealed to by Chinese parents regarding the careers of their sons.

1. Sheila Keppel, *China in 1700: Kangxi Porcelains at the Taft Museum*, exh. cat., Cincinnati, 1988, p. 12.

Provenance [Duveen, New York]; Taft collection, May 4, 1905.

1931.33

1931.33 view of back

Exhibition Cincinnati, Taft Museum [also Flint, Mich., and Muncie, Ind.], *China in 1700: Kangxi Porcelains at the Taft Museum,* Sept. 8, 1988–Sept. 17, 1989 (cat. by Sheila Keppel, no. 47).

Literature *Catalogue of the Taft Museum,* Cincinnati, 1939 and 1958, no. 358.

1931.33

Guanyin, Bodhisattva of Mercy

Kangxi reign (Qing dynasty), ca. 1700
Porcelain, H. 35.5 cm (14 in.)
Marks on back: *zhu* and *hua*

This famille verte figure of Guanyin, the bodhisattva of mercy, is seated cross-legged on an open lotus set on a galleried, pierced hexagonal stand. The child on her knee holds a lotus. The figure is enameled on the biscuit with floral patterns on her robes and a carp in a lobed panel on the formal, patterned grounds of the base. Traces of the extensive original red and black gouache remain on the unglazed areas. The back is decorated with penciled bamboo; lotus; and a pearl and a lozenge, two of the *babao,* or Eight Precious Things (see 1931.49, p. 617). The *zhu,* or pearl, and the *hua,* or lozenge representing a painting, mean "purity and perfection" and "wealth in art" respectively; hence this figure was highly esteemed by its maker. The square-cut aperture in the figure's back that was necessary for hollow firing was perhaps used to hold dedications and prayers.

This manifestation of Guanyin as the Songzu Guanyin, or "Bringer of Sons," appears in Chinese iconography soon after the arrival of Jesuit priests, who introduced Christianity in China. Visually this manifestation is expressed through the boy holding a lotus seated on Guanyin's knee, whose name is a homophone for *lianze,* or a wish for "continuous," or successive generations, of sons.

The carp painted on the base is a traditional symbol of fertility. It also represents a wish for sons to pass the civil-service examination. In Chinese mythology, when the fish leaps out of the waters of the Yellow River, crossing the threshold of the Dragon's Gate in the Henan province, it changes instantly into a dragon. This metamorphosis has become a visual metaphor for a successful candidate, or *jinshi,* departing the civil-service examination.

During the reign of the Kangxi emperor, when this figure was produced, Guanyin appeared in as many as five hundred different manifestations. One of the eight bodhisattvas, or contemporaries of Buddha in India during the end of the sixth or beginning of the fifth century B.C., Guanyin, historically a male prince, is the bodhisattva Avalokiteśvara, or lord of mercy. As did the other seven bodhisattvas, Avalokiteśvara delayed his own spiritual enlightenment to remain on earth, combining the spiritual virtues of the male and female sexes to alleviate the sufferings of humankind. As Buddhism spread throughout the Asiatic continent, following the trade routes, representations of this bejeweled Indian prince became increasingly feminine until Avalokiteśvara was commonly depicted as the beautiful and graceful Guanyin, or goddess of mercy.

Another popular manifestation of Guanyin, also found throughout Southeast Asia, is associated with the Amida cult and depicts the goddess seated on a lotus, referring to the legend that

1931.44, 49 detail of marks

1931.44, 49

she arrived at the island of Putuo in a boat made of lotus blossoms, offering rebirth into the Western Paradise (see 1931.168, p. 683).[1] Further explanations regarding the manifestation of Guanyin are found in Chinese legends. The goddess of mercy is said to be the daughter of a Zhou dynasty (ca. 1030–221 B.C.) ruler who was executed at her father's order for refusing to marry, as well as the daughter of an Indian prince who, as a pious follower of Buddha, converted her blind father by restoring his sight.[2]

1. Sheila Keppel, *China in 1700: Kangxi Porcelains at the Taft Museum,* exh. cat., Cincinnati, 1988, p. 11.

2. C. A. S. Williams, *Outlines of Chinese Symbolism and Art Motives,* New York, 1976, pp. 242–44.

Provenance [Duveen, New York]; Taft collection, Apr. 5, 1910.

Exhibition Cincinnati, Taft Museum [also Flint, Mich., and Muncie, Ind.], *China in 1700: Kangxi Porcelains at the Taft Museum,* Sept. 8, 1988–Sept. 17, 1989 (cat. by Sheila Keppel, no. 35).

Literature *Catalogue of the Taft Museum,* Cincinnati, 1939 and 1958, no. 351.

1931.44

Guanyin, Bodhisattva of Mercy

Kangxi reign (Qing dynasty), ca. 1700
Porcelain, H. 37.2 cm (14⅝ in.)
Mark (on back): *hua*

This famille verte figure of Guanyin, the bodhisattva of mercy, is seated cross-legged on an open lotus set on a balustraded, pierced hexagonal stand. The small boy on her right knee holds a lotus. The figure is enameled on the biscuit: her layered, flowered, and brocaded robes are reserved with landscape roundels in greens, mustard yellow, aubergine, and black. Traces of the extensive original cinnabar red gouache remain on the unglazed biscuit. The back is decorated with penciled bamboo; lotus; and a *hua* (a lozenge representing a painting), one of the *babao,* or Eight Precious Things.

The square-cut aperture in the back was necessary for hollow firing but was perhaps used to hold prayer papers.

This manifestation of Guanyin represents the Songzu Guanyin, the giver of children. Guanyin translates as "he who listens to the sounds (of the world)," referring to the bodhisattva Avalokiteśvara's historical role as a male Buddhist saint. Guanyin, the patron saint of Tibetan Buddhism, is believed to be reincarnated as the Dalai Lama.[1]

1. Wolfram Eberhard, *A Dictionary of Chinese Symbols,* trans. G. L. Campbell, London, 1991, p. 135.

Provenance [Duveen, New York]; Taft collection, Apr. 5, 1910.

Literature *Catalogue of the Taft Museum,* Cincinnati, 1939 and 1958, no. 342.

1931.49

1931.35, 42, 40, 37

Four Daoist Immortals

Kangxi reign (Qing dynasty), ca. 1700
Porcelain: 1931.35, H. 30.8 cm (12⅛ in.); 1931.42, H. 30.8 cm (12⅛ in.); 1931.40, H. 30 cm (11¾ in.); 1931.37, H. 30.5 cm (12 in.)
Unmarked

Each of these four famille verte figures of Daoist Immortals, from a house altar set of eight, is enameled on the biscuit and modeled standing on a table base draped with a cloth decorated with *shou,* or longevity, characters. All the figures bear traces of the original cinnabar red gouache on the unglazed biscuit areas.

Lu Dongbin (1931.35), a sage warrior who lived during the Tang dynasty (A.D. 618–906), is depicted holding a fly whisk, referring to his later role as patron of barbers. His checkerboard robe is reserved with floral roundels in aubergine, yellow, greens, and black.

Lan Caihe (1931.42), the patron of gardeners who was able to make plants grow and blossom, is depicted holding a flower basket. Her yellow coat is decorated with prunus roundels and *shou* characters. Historically a man, Lan Caihe appears in popular representations as a woman, warning against the fleeting pleasures of material life.

Han Xiangzi (1931.40), the patron of musicians, is shown holding a bamboo flute. His robes are enameled in colors with butterflies among scattered flower sprays. A favorite student of Lu Dongbin (1931.35), Han Xiangzi became an Immortal after his mentor took him to the supernatural peach tree of longevity that grows in the garden of Xi Wangmu, Queen Mother of the West.

1931.37 base of Cao Guojiu figure with instructions for proper placement when installing the household altar set

Cao Guojiu (1931.37), by legend the brother of a Song dynasty (A.D. 960–1279) empress and the maternal uncle of an emperor, is wearing a black court hat and holding two castanets, referring to his role as patron of actors. His robes are decorated with yellow and aubergine dragons on a green ground.

Missing from this altar set are the following four Daoist Immortals: Zhongli Chuan, chief of the Immortals, who is typically depicted holding the peach of immortality and a fan with which he revives the dead; Zhang Guolao, a recluse and magician of the Tang dynasty, who carries a bamboo fish drum and two metal rods with which to beat upon it, representing his ability to foretell the future; Li Tieguai, a lame beggar who leans on an iron crutch and carries a bottle gourd emblematic of his magical drugs that relieve suffering; and He Xiangu, a Tang dynasty daughter of a merchant who ate the peach of immortality. The patron of households, her emblem is the lotus, a symbol associated with marriage.

Provenance James A. Garland, New York; J. Pierpont Morgan, New York (in 1911); [Duveen, New York]; Taft collection, Apr. 30, 1915.

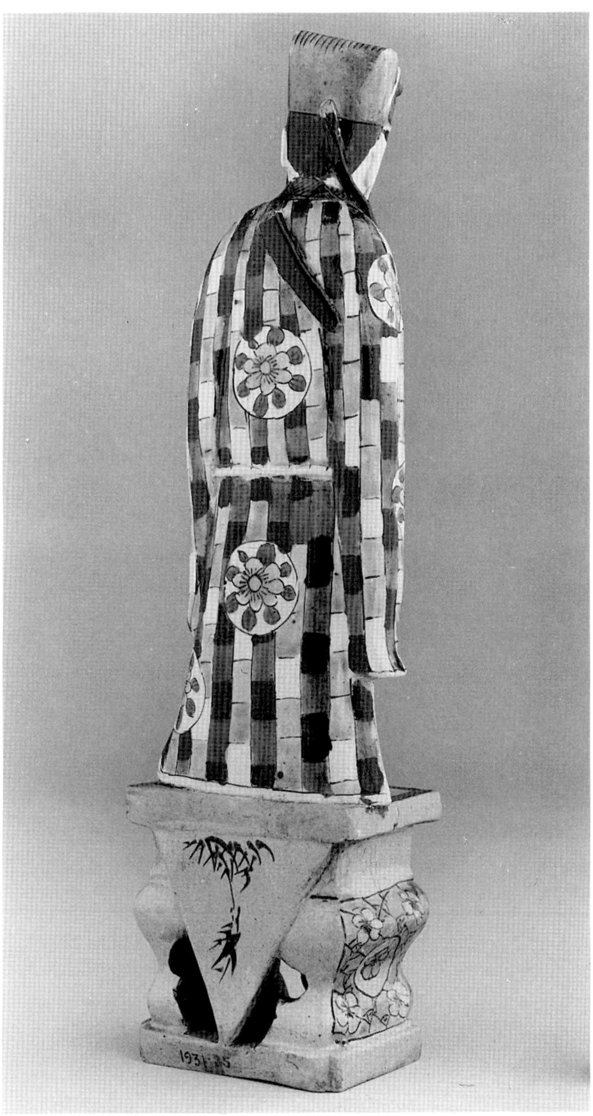

1931.35 Lu Dongbin, reverse

Exhibition Cincinnati, Taft Museum [also Flint, Mich. and Muncie, Ind.], *China in 1700: Kangxi Porcelains at the Taft Museum,* Sept. 8, 1988–Sept. 17, 1989 (cat. by Sheila Keppel, nos. 36–39).

Literature J. Pierpont Morgan, *Catalogue of the Morgan Collection of Chinese Porcelains,* vol. II, New York, 1911, nos. 1167–70; *Catalogue of the Taft Museum,* Cincinnati, 1939 and 1958, nos. 328–31.

1931.35, 1931.42, 1931.40, 1931.37

1931.28

Figure of a Civil Mandarin

Kangxi reign (Qing dynasty), ca. 1700
Porcelain, H. 21 cm (8¼ in.)
Unmarked

This famille verte figure of a first-grade mandarin is depicted sitting on a stepped, flowered throne and wearing layered robes enameled in colors with crane roundels, scattered flower branches, and formal patterns on an aubergine ground. His finely modeled head has tiny apertures for hair whiskers (now missing; see 1931.33, p. 615, for an intact example). The back is drilled with a hole through a *shou* medallion.

Originally this figure would have held a *hu,* or tablet-shaped scepter, emblematic of his civil mandarin rank (now missing; see the following figure for an intact example).

Provenance [Duveen, New York (as early Kangxi)]; Taft collection, Nov. 10, 1905.

Literature *Catalogue of the Taft Museum,* Cincinnati, 1939 and 1958, no. 326.

1931.28

Figure of a Civil Mandarin

Kangxi reign (Qing dynasty), ca. 1700
Porcelain, H. 21 cm (8¼ in.)
Unmarked

This famille verte figure of a first-grade civil mandarin is seated on a stepped flower throne and holds a *hu,* or tablet-shaped scepter, representing his rank. His head has been replaced with a contemporary blanc-de-chine head from Dehua in Fujian province of a smiling Luohan, a Buddhist ascetic monk. The robes of the figure are elaborately enameled in colors with crane roundels among fruiting peach sprays on a lime green ground.

During the early twentieth century, restorers used genuine parts of period Chinese ceramics when repairing damaged objects. Compare, for example, this figure to its companion piece (the preceding example), which is unaltered but is missing his tablet of rank.

1931.24

Provenance [Duveen, New York (as pair with 1931.28)]; Taft collection, Nov. 10, 1905.

Literature *Catalogue of the Taft Museum,* Cincinnati, 1939 and 1958, no. 322.

1931.24

1931.31

Figure of a Civil Mandarin

Kangxi reign (Qing dynasty), ca. 1700
Porcelain, H. 22.2 cm. (8¾ in.)
Unmarked

This famille verte figure of a first-grade civil mandarin is depicted with a well-modeled laughing small boy riding piggyback, enameled in colors and gilt. The man is wearing a flowered tunic with the mandarin square of the flying crane over a long robe decorated with cranes among clouds; the boy wears a patchwork coat reserved with lion and chrysanthemum roundels.

Fu Xing, one of the Three Star Gods of Daoism and the god of blessings (see 1931.82, p. 632), is often depicted wearing a robe with a mandarin square and carrying a boy on his back.[1] This representation refers to the strong desire of Chinese parents for male offspring.

1. See William R. Sargent, *The Copeland Collection*, Salem, Mass., 1991, p. 103, no. 47, for a similar example.

Provenance [Parish-Watson, New York]; Taft collection, Apr. 14, 1924.

Exhibition Cincinnati, Taft Museum, *Ming to Ch'ing: Imperial Objects and Textiles, Masterpieces of Chinese Furniture*, Feb. 12–June 30, 1975.

Literature *Catalogue of the Taft Museum*, Cincinnati, 1939 and 1958, no. 336.

1931.31

1931.31 view of back

1931.25

Boy Astride a Qilin

Kangxi reign (Qing dynasty), 1662–1722
Porcelain, H. 19 cm (7½ in.)
Unmarked

This famille verte figure is of a small boy astride a *qilin*. He is laughing and holding a *sheng*, or reed pipe, in one hand and a lotus branch in the other. The figure's tunic is reserved in green, black, iron red, and yellow with loose peony flowers.[1]

The Chinese believe that auspicious symbols, either written out entirely or expressed visually by rebuses, or pictorial puns, can assist in making their wishes come true. Since so many words in Chinese are homophonous, figures such as this one can be interpreted as visual plays on words. The combination of a boy holding a reed pipe while seated on a *qilin*, a composite mythical beast that delivers baby boys much like the Western stork,[2] represents the wish for male offspring. The reed pipe, or *sheng*, is a homophone for "to give birth," and the lotus branch, or *lian*, also means "continuous."[3] When combined with the *qilin*, they express a wish for successive generations of sons.

This figure is similar to one of a pair of figures (the other an older man wearing a straw hat) sold in London in 1970.[4]

1. According to the Apr. 30, 1915, invoice from Duveen Brothers, this figure was formerly in the collections of James A. Garland and J. Pierpont Morgan. Although this object was listed as number 1527 in the Morgan collection, J. Pierpont Morgan's *Catalogue of the Morgan Collection of Chinese Porcelains* (vol. II, New York, 1911) ends with entry number 1521. The figure also does not appear in John Getz's catalogue of the Garland collection.

2. Terese Tse Bartholomew, *Myths and Rebuses in Chinese Art,* exh. cat., Asian Art Museum of San Francisco, 1988, n.p.

3. Sheila Keppel, *China in 1700: Kangxi Porcelains at the Taft Museum,* exh. cat., Cincinnati, 1988, p. 16.

4. Sale, Christie's, London, *Property of the Late A. C. J. Wall,* Oct. 5, 1970, no. 160.

Provenance James A. Garland, New York (according to Duveen invoice); [Duveen, New York, 1902]; J. Pierpont Morgan, New York (cat. no. 1527, according to Duveen invoice); [Duveen, New York]; Taft collection, Apr. 30, 1915.

Exhibition Cincinnati, Taft Museum [also Flint, Mich., and Muncie, Ind.], *China in 1700: Kangxi Porcelains at the Taft Museum,* Sept. 8, 1988–Sept. 17, 1989 (cat. by Sheila Keppel, no. 73).

Literature *Catalogue of the Taft Museum,* Cincinnati, 1939 and 1958, no. 283 (ill.).

1931.25

Figure of a Laughing Small Boy

Kangxi reign (Qing dynasty), ca. 1700
Porcelain, H. 15.9 cm (6¼ in.)
Unmarked

This famille verte figure of a laughing small boy, modeled in a seated position with his legs apart, wears rings around his ankles and a short tunic enameled on the biscuit with colored and gilt flower sprays on a turquoise ground.

Figures of seated boys such as this example may have been intended as presents for Chinese couples who were hoping for male children.

1931.26

Provenance [Duveen, New York]; Taft collection, May 4, 1905.

Exhibition Cincinnati, Taft Museum, *Ming to Ch'ing: Imperial Objects and Textiles, Masterpieces of Chinese Furniture,* Feb. 12–June 30, 1975.

Literature *Catalogue of the Taft Museum,* Cincinnati, 1939 and 1958, no. 344.

1931.26

Asil Game Cockerel

Kangxi reign (Qing dynasty), ca. 1700
Porcelain, H. 26.7 cm (10½ in.)
Unmarked

This famille verte cockerel is modeled perched astride a pierced outcrop of rock. The crisply molded biscuit is enameled in a typical famille verte palette of yellow, leaf green, pale aubergine, and turquoise and is detailed in black. The wattle and comb are in iron red with gilt.

The asil game cockerel is the oldest pure breed of domestic poultry. The cockscomb, which is a pun for *guan,* or the hat of an official, is associated with wishes for advancement in civil service.[1]

1. Terese Tse Bartholomew, *Myths and Rebuses in Chinese Art,* exh. cat., Asian Art Museum of San Francisco, 1988, n.p.

1931.45

Provenance James A. Garland, New York; [Duveen, New York, 1902]; J. Pierpont Morgan, New York (in 1904); [Duveen, New York]; Taft collection, Apr. 30, 1915.

Literature Robert Grier Cooke, *Catalogue of the Morgan Collection of Chinese Porcelains,* vol. 1, New York, 1904, p. 106, no. 679; *Catalogue of the Taft Museum,* Cincinnati, 1939 and 1958, no. 360.

1931.45

1948.1–2

Pair of Buddhistic Lions

Kangxi reign (Qing dynasty), ca. 1700–1720
Porcelain, H. (each) 46.3 cm (18¼ in.)
Unmarked

Each figure of this pair of famille verte Buddhistic lions is modeled sitting on a flowered rectangular base. Both are enameled in colors and gilt with green bodies, aubergine manes and tails, and blue conical hair curls. The female, looking to her right, is depicted with a yellow-bodied cub clambering onto her. The male, facing to the left, rests his left paw on a ball decorated with loose flowers.

The great interest in Buddhistic lions during the Qing dynasty (1644–1912) arose when the Manchu people were struggling to retain their cultural identity while assimilating with the native Chinese society. In 1635 the Jürchen people, descendants of the Tungus tribes who had founded the Jin dynasty (1115–1234) in northeast China, renamed themselves Manchus (*Manzhou*) and began the conquest of the unstable Ming dynasty (1368–1644).[1] After the formation of the Qing dynasty in 1644, the Manchus depicted the Buddhistic lion in art more often than it had been in any preceding dynasty to emphasize their belief in Buddhism.

Depictions of the Buddhistic lion, or dog of Fo, conventionally resemble a dog rather than a lion. Sheila Keppel notes that the Pekinese dog was avidly bred during the seventeenth century to give prominence to its increasingly lionlike features. The Taft Buddhistic lions bear the Chinese character *wang,* an emblem of royal authority, on their foreheads to stress further an imperial connection with Buddhism. The ball under the male's foot may allude to the pearl of authority that the imperial dragon often chases.[2]

1. Jacques Gernet, *A History of Chinese Civilization,* trans. J. R. Foster, Cambridge (Eng.), 1990, p. 463.

2. Sheila Keppel, *China in 1700: Kangxi Porcelains at the Taft Museum,* exh. cat., Cincinnati, 1988, p. 7.

Provenance Richard Bennett, Thornby Hall, Northampton, Eng.; S. E. Kennedy, London; [Duveen, New York]; Edward T. Stotesbury, Chestnut Hill, Pa.; [Rosenberg & Stiebel, New York]; gift of Louise Taft Semple, Nov. 1948.

Exhibition Cincinnati, Taft Museum [also Flint, Mich., and Muncie, Ind.], *China in 1700: Kangxi Porcelains at the Taft Museum,* Sept. 8, 1988–Sept. 17, 1989 (cat. by Sheila Keppel, no. 24 [1948.2]).

Literature Edgar Gorer, *Catalogue of the Collection of Old Chinese Porcelains Formed by Richard Bennett, Esq.,* London, n.d., p. 65, no. 332 (color ill.); Edgar Gorer and J. F. Blacker, *Chinese Porcelains and Hard Stones,* vol. 1, London, 1911, pl. 83; *Prime Antiques and Their Current Prices,* ed. Thomas Hamilton Ormsbee, New York, 1947, p. 369, no. 1255; *Catalogue of the Taft Museum,* Cincinnati, 1958, nos. 435 A–B.

1948.1–2

1931.29

Candlestick

Kangxi reign (Qing dynasty), 1662–1722
Porcelain, H. 24.8 cm (9¾ in.)
Unmarked

This biscuit famille verte candlestick is modeled as a Luohan, a Buddhist ascetic monk, squatting on a low hexagonal table stand draped with a cloth decorated with cranes, symbolizing immortality, and the *shou,* or long-life character. The figure holds a lotus waxpan on his head with both hands and wears wide-sleeved robes enameled with *guilong,* or serpentine dragons, gamboling among scrolling lotus on a green ground.

The eighteen Luohans, disciples of Buddha, are identified by individual symbols; the waxpan held by this figure of Nagaxian resembles his attribute, a Buddhistic begging bowl.

Provenance Richard Bennett, Thornby Hall, Northampton, Eng.; [Parish-Watson, New York]; Taft collection, Oct. 30, 1924.

Literature Edgar Gorer, *Catalogue of the Collection of Old Chinese Porcelains Formed by Richard Bennett, Esq.,* London, n.d., pp. 57–58, no. 299, pl. opp. p. 59; *Catalogue of the Taft Museum,* Cincinnati, 1939 and 1958, no. 284.

1931.29

Two Figures of Standing Boys

Kangxi reign (Qing dynasty), ca. 1700–1720
Porcelain, H. (each) 29.5 cm (11⅝ in.)
Unmarked

These two famille verte figures of boys are modeled standing on rectangular rockwork bases and are now supporting on their right hands candle holders in the shape of lotus flowers resting on flowered cloths. Each is enameled in colors with flowered green tunics belted over yellow trousers tucked into black knee boots. One has a glazed aubergine face.

The lotus-flower candle holders are later additions, replacing the original simple cylindrical ones. It is possible that these figures represent stylized East Indians or Mongols.

Provenance [Duveen, New York]; Taft collection, May 4, 1905.

Literature *Catalogue of the Taft Museum,* Cincinnati, 1939 and 1958, nos. 300, 304.

1931.6, 1931.10

1931.6, 10

Pair of Brush Washers

Kangxi reign (Qing dynasty), ca. 1700
Porcelain, H. (each) 24.8 cm (9¾ in.)
Unmarked

Each of this pair of famille verte brush washers is modeled as a lakeside palace pavilion on a quatrefoil base. Both are enameled

1931.16, 20

on the biscuit in yellow, aubergine, and green with loose splashes of the egg-and-spinach pattern around the outside of the bases. One (1931.16) retains several traces of red gouache on the unglazed columns.

Originally, small figures (now detached from 1931.20 and missing from 1931.16) were crossing the bridge.

Provenance [Duveen, New York]; Taft collection, May 4, 1905.

Literature *Catalogue of the Taft Museum,* Cincinnati, 1939 and 1958, nos. 339, 348.

1931.16, 1931.20

Brush Washer

Kangxi reign (Qing dynasty), ca. 1700
Porcelain, H. 8 cm (3⅛ in.)
Unmarked

This famille verte brush washer is modeled as Li Daibo, reclining against his wine jar with a tablet in one hand. It is enameled on the biscuit in green, aubergine, yellow, and black and decorated with roundels of *guilong,* or serpentine dragons; landscapes on his robes; and prunus reserved in white on the green ground of his wine jar.

Li Daibo (699–762), a distant relative of the Tang emperors, is among the most celebrated of the Chinese poets. He is equally well known for his drunkenness, hence the wine jar.

Provenance [Duveen, New York]; Taft collection, May 4, 1905.

Exhibition Cincinnati, Taft Museum [also Flint, Mich., and Muncie, Ind.], *China in 1700: Kangxi Porcelains at the Taft Museum,* Sept. 8, 1988–Sept. 17, 1989 (cat. by Sheila Keppel, no. 58).

Literature *Catalogue of the Taft Museum,* Cincinnati, 1939 and 1958, no. 346.

1931.46

1931.46

1950.1–2

Pair of Water Droppers

Kangxi reign (Qing dynasty), ca. 1700
Porcelain: 1950.1, H. 10.8 cm (4¼ in.); 1950.2, H. 12.1 cm (4¾ in.)
Unmarked

These two famille verte water droppers are modeled as ponies, semirecumbent on green leaves. They are enameled on the biscuit: one with an aubergine body and yellow mane and tail; the other with a yellow body, piebald in sepia, white mane and tail, and aubergine hooves.

William Sargent compares the pose of these Mongolian ponies, forelegs extended against the green grounds as though struggling up from rest, to European models. Identically posed examples, executed in Delft tin-glazed earthenware, date from the late seventeenth century. Sargent suggests that Chinese prototypes may have been collected during the late seventeenth and early eighteenth centuries in the West, while Dutch models were also being sent to Japan for execution in porcelain and export to Europe.[1]

Noting the similarity of the posture of these ponies to the five-color cavalry horses Wang Maozhong offered as tribute gifts to the Xuanzong emperor (713–55), Sargent explains that the piebald pony may be a reference to the "Black Jade Piebald Horse" from the *Gu Yu Tu*.[2] Further, he explains that dappled horses were believed "to presage inspiration."[3]

Water droppers, such as this engaging pair of ponies, were used by scholars at their writing desks. After submerging the vessels to fill the hollow bodies, water was poured from the ponies' mouths; their tails served as handles.

1. William R. Sargent, *The Copeland Collection*, Salem, Mass., 1991, pp. 62–63, fig. 19.

2. Sargent, p. 62.

3. Sargent, p. 64, fig. 20.

Provenance Stephen Winkworth, London (sale, Sotheby's, London, 1933); [C. T. Loo, New York]; gift of Louise Taft Semple, June 22, 1950.

Exhibition Cincinnati, Taft Museum, *Ming to Ch'ing: Imperial Objects and Textiles, Masterpieces of Chinese Furniture,* Feb. 12–June 30, 1975.

Literature *Catalogue of the Taft Museum,* Cincinnati, 1958, nos. 293 A–B.

1950.1–2

Teapot

Kangxi reign (Qing dynasty), ca. 1700
Porcelain, H. 18.4 cm (7¼ in.)
Unmarked

This famille verte teapot is modeled as a small boy, wearing a gilt *ruyi* head around his neck, astride a recumbent *qilin.* His outstretched right hand holds a *sheng,* or reed pipe, forming the spout, while his left arm rests on the mythical beast's tail to form the handle. The stopper is the boy's top knot, which is mostly a replacement. The figure's tunic and trousers are enameled on the biscuit in colors and gilt with formal peony flowers on a lime green ground. The beast has a scaly aubergine body and yellow dragon head.

The rebus depicted on this teapot is nearly identical to that on 1931.25 (p. 621), expressing the wish for male offspring. In this instance, however, the *ruyi*-head necklace that the boy wears places additional emphasis on the pun, since *ruyi* means "as you wish."[1]

1. Terese Tse Bartholomew, *Myths and Rebuses in Chinese Art,* exh. cat., Asian Art Museum of San Francisco, 1988, n.p.

1931.27

Provenance James A. Garland, New York; [Duveen, New York, 1902]; J. Pierpont Morgan, New York (in 1904); [Duveen, New York]; Taft collection, Apr. 30, 1915.

Literature Robert Grier Cooke, *Catalogue of the Morgan Collection of Chinese Porcelains,* vol. 1, New York, 1904, p. 96, no. 593; *Catalogue of the Taft Museum,* Cincinnati, 1939 and 1958, no. 285.

1931.27

Teapot with Flat Cover

Kangxi reign (Qing dynasty), 1662–1722
Porcelain, H. 9.5 cm (3¾ in.)
Unmarked

This famille verte teapot with flat cover is molded as a cylindrical cluster of bamboo canes with a loop handle and shaped spout. It is enameled in colors on the biscuit with panels of birds, flowers, fruit, and fungus in aubergine, greens, yellow, turquoise, and black on contrasting grounds from the same palette.

Provenance [Duveen, New York]; Taft collection, Oct. 27, 1902.

Literature John Getz, *A Catalogue of Chinese Porcelains Collected by Mr. and Mrs. Charles P. Taft,* New York, 1904, no. 52; *Catalogue of the Taft Museum,* Cincinnati, 1939 and 1958, no. 323.

1931.76

1931.76

1931.8

Teapot with Domed Cover

Kangxi reign (Qing dynasty), ca. 1680–1700
Porcelain, H. 18.7 cm (7⅜ in.)
Unmarked

This famille verte hexagonal teapot with domed cover has a slender body with reticulated panels and is modeled with a bamboo handle, spout, and borders to each side. The sides and domed cover are set with openwork panels of flowering branches.

The flat shoulder is decorated with two of the *babao,* or Eight Precious Things — the pearl representing perfection, the artemisia leaf representing dignity — repeated on a green brocade ground. The whole is enameled on the biscuit in colors.

Provenance [Duveen, New York]; Taft collection, Nov. 5, 1903.

Literature John Getz, *A Catalogue of Chinese Porcelains Collected by Mr. and Mrs. Charles P. Taft,* New York, 1904, no. 53; *Catalogue of the Taft Museum,* Cincinnati, 1939 and 1958, no. 347.

1931.8

Teapot with Cover

Kangxi reign (Qing dynasty), ca. 1700
Porcelain, H. 15.2 cm (6 in.)
Unmarked

This famille verte globular teapot with cover is modeled as bamboo with each cane variously enameled in colors with birds, flowers, and bamboo. The spout is in the shape of a gnarled branch, and the square loop handle is molded and incised to resemble wrapped bamboo cane.

Provenance [Duveen, New York]; Taft collection, Oct. 27, 1902.

Literature John Getz, *A Catalogue of Chinese Porcelains Collected by Mr. and Mrs. Charles P. Taft,* New York, 1904, no. 47; *Catalogue of the Taft Museum,* Cincinnati, 1939 and 1958, no. 340.

1931.75

1931.75

1931.73

Teapot with Cover

Kangxi reign (Qing dynasty), ca. 1700
Porcelain, H. 15 cm (5⅞ in.)
Unmarked

This famille verte hexagonal teapot with cover has a slender body with sides resembling the shape of an open book, a shaped spout, and a yellow squared handle, molded and incised to resemble wrapped bamboo cane. It is enameled on the biscuit with landscape vignettes on yellow flowered grounds and with panels of flowering branches on white and yellow grounds.

Provenance [Duveen, New York]; Taft collection, Mar. 28, 1908.

Exhibition Cincinnati, Taft Museum [also Flint, Mich., and Muncie, Ind.], *China in 1700: Kangxi Porcelains at the Taft Museum,* Sept. 8, 1988–Sept. 17, 1989 (cat. by Sheila Keppel, no. 27).

Literature *Catalogue of the Taft Museum,* Cincinnati, 1939 and 1958, no. 349.

1931.73

Teapot with Flat Cover

Kangxi reign (Qing dynasty), ca. 1700
Porcelain, H. 11.5 cm (4½ in.)
Mark: underglaze blue ribboned fly

This famille verte teapot with flat cover is molded as a cluster of bamboo with a gnarled stem spout, loop handle, and twig

1931.3

finial. It is enameled in bright colors with panels of yellow cockerels and branches of chrysanthemum, prunus, and other flowers. The spout, handle, and finial are decorated with scattered branches, and the cover with four cockerels.

Provenance [Duveen, New York]; Taft collection, Dec. 12, 1902.

Literature John Getz, *A Catalogue of Chinese Porcelains Collected by Mr. and Mrs. Charles P. Taft,* New York, 1904, no. 51; *Catalogue of the Taft Museum,* Cincinnati, 1939 and 1958, no. 325.

1931.3

Bay-lep

Kangxi reign (Qing dynasty), ca. 1662–80
Porcelain, H. 42.7 cm (16¾ in.)
Unmarked

This famille verte cylindrical *bay-lep,* a milk jug or yak-milk ewer, in the form of a section of bamboo has a horizontally ribbed body with lion-mask loops for a rope handle facing each other on the side opposite to the monstrous-headed shaped spout and the lip with a diadem above the spout. It is enameled in aubergine, yellow, dark and pale green, and clear white on the biscuit with eleven mythical seahorses, or *hai-mu,* galloping above rocks and waves scattered with *babao,* or the Eight Precious Things, and flower heads all on a ground of green swirling waves breaking on rocks in three panels. The spout is decorated with flames, and the diadem lip with a crane among clouds.[1]

1. See John Ayers, *Chinese Ceramics: The Kroger Collection,* London, 1985, p. 124, no. 98, pl. p. 125, for a nearly identical example.

Provenance Ivor Bertie Guest, first baron Wimborne; [Duveen, New York (as "Ming period")]; Taft collection, Nov. 5, 1903.

1931.93

Literature John Getz, *A Catalogue of Chinese Porcelains Collected by Mr. and Mrs. Charles P. Taft,* New York, 1904, no. 67; *Catalogue of the Taft Museum,* Cincinnati, 1939 and 1958, no. 422.

1931.93

1931.192

Ewer with Domed Cover

Kangxi reign (Qing dynasty), ca. 1700
Porcelain, H. 35.6 cm (14 in.)
Unmarked, but with underglaze blue cross and parallel lines on the lip of the ewer for matching body to cover.

The form of this famille verte hexagonal pear-shaped ewer with domed cover has been taken directly from Near Eastern metalwork, with a faceted body set on a flaring hexagonal base, a tall hexagonal spout and scrolled handle with finger and thumb grips, and a domed, faceted cover with a crouching Buddhistic lion finial. The ewer is enameled in colors with principal panels of phoenix and pheasant among pierced rockwork as well as flowering tree peonies and prunus branches on a ground of loose flower and foliage scrolls. The spout and handle are enameled with scattered flowers and leaves.

This particular Islamic metalwork shape was produced in ceramics not only in China during the Kangxi period but also in Japan during the late seventeenth century for export to the West.

Provenance [Duveen, New York]; Taft collection, May 4, 1905.

Literature *Catalogue of the Taft Museum,* Cincinnati, 1939 and 1958, no. 363.

1931.192

1931.72

Basket with Domed Cover

Kangxi reign (Qing dynasty), ca. 1700
Porcelain, H. 12 cm (4¾ in.)
Unmarked

This famille verte reticulated basket consists of a compressed globular body and shallow domed cover with enameled and lightly molded chrysanthemum sprays on yellow openwork cell-pattern grounds. The squared loop handle is incised and enameled to resemble wrapped canework; the neck, with iron red breaking waves. The finial is modeled as a diminutive standing Buddhistic lion.[1]

This covered basket was probably used to hold potpourri or as a cage for singing crickets.

1. See Edgar Gorer and J. F. Blacker, *Chinese Porcelains and Hard Stones,* vol. II, London, 1911, pl. 184, for an identical example.

Provenance [Duveen, New York]; Taft collection, Nov. 27, 1902.

Literature John Getz, *A Catalogue of Chinese Porcelains Collected by Mr. and Mrs. Charles P. Taft,* New York, 1904, no. 49; *Catalogue of the Taft Museum,* Cincinnati, 1939 and 1958, no. 338.

1931.72

Hanging Flower Vase

Kangxi reign (Qing dynasty), ca. 1700
Porcelain, H. 29.2 cm (11½ in.)
Unmarked

This famille verte reticulated hanging flower vase has an openwork oviform body carved with bands of endless knots; the base

1931.7

1931.9

is pierced with a cash pattern. The wide sloping lip is enameled in colors with peony, lotus, and prunus blossoms on formal patterned grounds. The *faux bois* flattened yoke is joined to the basket by two seven-link luted chains. The basket is set with a liner beaker decorated with a prunus-on-cracked-ice border.

The endless knot, or *pan zhang*, is one of the *ba jixiang*, or Eight Buddhist Symbols. A popular ornamental motif in China, it is also known as the lucky knot and symbolizes long life without disappointments.

Provenance [Duveen, New York]; Taft collection, Oct. 21, 1902.

Literature John Getz, *A Catalogue of Chinese Porcelains Collected by Mr. and Mrs. Charles P. Taft*, New York, 1904, no. 41; *Catalogue of the Taft Museum*, Cincinnati, 1939 and 1958, no. 369.

1931.7

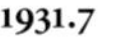

Hanging Flower Vase

Kangxi reign (Qing dynasty), ca. 1700
Porcelain, H. 29.8 cm (11¾ in.)
Unmarked

This famille verte reticulated hanging flower vase has a carved openwork oviform body composed of bands of endless knots divided by bands with scattered flower heads enameled in green, yellow, iron red, and pale aubergine. The base is enameled with flowers and butterflies, centered on a pierced cash pattern. The outside of the wide lip is decorated with *ruyi* lappets; the inside with a band of lotus, chrysanthemum, prunus, and tree-peony flowers on a seeded green ground. A butterfly is set on each side of the lip near an iron-red-and-gilt hook. Seven iron red porcelain links — fired and attached to each side of a flattened yoke,

1931.9 detail of base

which is enameled with flowers on a seeded green ground—suspend the vase.

One ring is now repaired in metal. The flower holder, a cylindrical liner beaker originally placed inside the basket, is missing (see the preceding vase for an intact example).

Provenance [Duveen, New York]; Taft collection, Oct. 21, 1902.

Literature John Getz, *A Catalogue of Chinese Porcelains Collected by Mr. and Mrs. Charles P. Taft,* New York, 1904, no. 40; *Catalogue of the Taft Museum,* Cincinnati, 1939 and 1958, no. 367.

1931.9

Pastille Burner, or Candle Lantern

Kangxi reign (Qing dynasty), ca. 1700
Porcelain, H. 21 cm (8¼ in.)
Unmarked

This famille verte openwork hexagonal pastille burner, or candle lantern, sits on a shallow base. The thin slab sides and flat top of the cover are cut with swastikas set on the same diagonal as the main panels. It is enameled with iron red flower heads scattered on leaf green and black brocade grounds. The stand has six short bracket feet.

The swastika is a Buddhist motif that came from India with the religion. It was thought to deflect evil with its crossed counter-directional lines and also serves as a rebus in Chinese for *wan,* or ten thousand.

Provenance [Duveen, New York]; Taft collection, Apr. 28, 1902.

Literature John Getz, *A Catalogue of Chinese Porcelains Collected by Mr. and Mrs. Charles P. Taft,* New York, 1904, no. 55; *Catalogue of the Taft Museum,* Cincinnati, 1939 and 1958, no. 324.

1931.41

Lantern Shade

Kangxi reign (Qing dynasty), ca. 1700
Porcelain, H. 21.4 cm (8⅜ in.)
Unmarked

This famille verte plain oviform eggshell lantern shade is enameled in colors and gilt with the Three Star Gods of Daoism accompanied by attendants and small boys on a terrace: Shou Xing, or Shoulao, the god of longevity, wearing a light green robe and grasping his staff, and accompanied by an attendant bearing a peach of immortality; Lu Xing, the god of rank and emolument, wearing an orange brocaded robe and black court hat and holding his ivory scepter; and Fu Xing, the god of blessings, wearing a light green robe, standing with his usual attribute, a child who holds a *sheng,* or reed pipe, referring to the primary Chinese wish for male offspring. The shoulders and cylindrical collar are decorated with formal and floral bands on aubergine scroll-pattern grounds. The base repeats the decoration of the neck.

The stepped candle stand is missing.

1931.41

1931.82 Lu Xing (left), Fu Xing (right)

1931.82

The representation of the Three Star Gods of Daoism is a rebus for the phrase *Fu-lu-shou san-shing,* a basic Chinese wish for blessings (specifically children), rank, and longevity.

Provenance [Parish-Watson, New York (as "perfect")]; Taft collection, Apr. 14, 1924.

Literature *Catalogue of the Taft Museum,* Cincinnati, 1939 and 1958, no. 354.

1931.82

Lantern

Kangxi reign (Qing dynasty), ca. 1720
Porcelain, H. 31.8 cm (12½ in.)
Unmarked

This famille verte hexagonal lantern is enameled with six male foreigners, each riding a fanciful beast in a landscape and probably bearing a tribute gift. The collars at the top and bottom are decorated with shaped panels of crustaceans on formal patterned grounds. The spreading lip and separate base are open fretwork enameled in green and iron red.

During the Qing dynasty, especially in the eighteenth century, a fairly common decorative motif was that of foreign barbarians bringing tribute gifts to the Manchu emperor. The six figures are depicted on mythical animals that are unrelated to typical Chinese pictorial conventions deliberately to heighten the exotic appeal of the motif.[1]

1931.84

1. I am grateful to the late Schuyler Cammon for his assistance in identifying this motif.

Provenance [Duveen, New York (as "repaired")]; Taft collection, Apr. 23, 1910.

Literature *Catalogue of the Taft Museum,* Cincinnati, 1939 and 1958, no. 368.

1931.84

Lantern

Kangxi reign (Qing dynasty), ca. 1700
Porcelain, H. 22.8 cm (9 in.)
Unmarked

This famille verte plain oviform eggshell lantern is enameled in colors and gilt and depicts an elaborate audience scene on a terrace in front of rockwork and a swirling vortex. Surrounded by attendants carrying banners decorated with trigrams, an archer bows to the seated military commander. The shoulders and cylindrical collars are decorated with lotus branches and panels of the Four Liberal Accomplishments on floral grounds above and *ruyi* lappets below. The base repeats the decoration of the neck. The candle stand is missing.

1931.86

The swirling vortex and rockwork behind the military commander are longevity symbols, perhaps indicating that the scene takes place near the Eastern Sea. Or, these motifs may refer to the *shan men hai shi* (the mountain-oath and the sea-oath), a sacred vow symbolizing China as a whole.[1] The commander wears a robe that displays the crane in a mandarin square, indicating his rank as a fourth-grade official.

Although precise identification of this subject remains to be documented, the audience scene may be based on the fourteenth-century epic novel *Sanguozhi Yanyi,* or *The Romance of the Three Kingdoms* (see 1931.159, p. 639). One possible explanation is that the seated military commander is Liu Bei, a member of the Han imperial family, who attempted to reunite his country during the third century A.D., when the Han dynasty (206 B.C.–A.D. 220) empire disintegrated and China was splintered into the Three Kingdoms (A.D. 220–65).

1. Wolfram Eberhard, *A Dictionary of Chinese Symbols,* trans. G. L. Campbell, London, 1991, p. 196.

Provenance [Parish-Watson, New York (as Kangxi)]; Taft collection, Apr. 14, 1924.

Exhibition Cincinnati, Taft Museum [also Flint, Mich., and Muncie, Ind.], *China in 1700: Kangxi Porcelains at the Taft Museum,* Sept. 8, 1988–Sept. 17, 1989 (cat. by Sheila Keppel, no. 40).

Literature *Catalogue of the Taft Museum,* Cincinnati, 1939 and 1958, no. 345.

1931.86

1931.86 three attendants carrying banners, behind archer

1931.86 three attendants carrying banners, to right of audience tent

1931.87, 91

Pair of Rouleau Vases

Kangxi reign (Qing dynasty), ca. 1700
Porcelain: 1931.87, H. 28.8 cm (11⅜ in.); 1931.91, H. 28.3 cm (11⅛ in.)
Mark: underglaze blue double ring

This pair of famille verte rouleau vases with short trumpet necks is enameled in colors with four wide bands on alternating grounds of lime green and iron red. Interlocking formal flowering foliage scrolls on lime green grounds with *ruyi* head panels in yellow make up the top band. *Guilong,* or serpentine dragons, chase flaming pearls on a bright iron red ground directly below. The rounded shoulders are decorated with flowered zigzags in yellow, lime green, and iron red, and the necks and bases with stiff green leaves on iron red grounds.

This type of vase was extremely popular with eighteenth-century collectors, who often had this shape mounted in ormolu. These rouleau vases are closely related in shape, size, and decoration to 1931.68 (p. 588).

Provenance [Duveen, New York]; Taft collection, May 4, 1905.

Literature *Catalogue of the Taft Museum,* Cincinnati, 1939 and 1958, nos. 366, 370.

1931.87, 1931.91

Rouleau Vase

Kangxi reign (Qing dynasty), ca. 1700
Porcelain, H. 46.3 cm (18¼ in.)
Mark: underglaze blue double ring

This famille verte rouleau vase is enameled in colors with a kingfisher perched on the stalk of an old, molding leaf in a lotus pond with buds; full-blown iron red and aubergine flowers; and

1931.142

1931.161

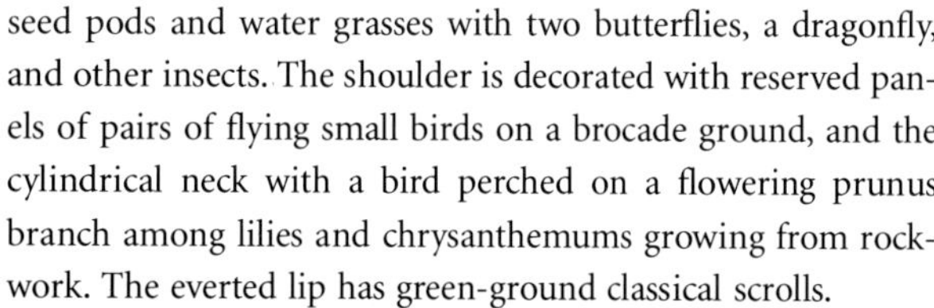

seed pods and water grasses with two butterflies, a dragonfly, and other insects. The shoulder is decorated with reserved panels of pairs of flying small birds on a brocade ground, and the cylindrical neck with a bird perched on a flowering prunus branch among lilies and chrysanthemums growing from rockwork. The everted lip has green-ground classical scrolls.

The enameling on this vase, particularly the layered shading of the decaying lotus leaf, is of superb quality.

Provenance Edward R. Bacon, New York (in 1919); [Parish-Watson, New York]; Taft collection, Nov. 9, 1923.

Exhibition Cincinnati, Taft Museum [also Flint, Mich., and Muncie, Ind.], *China in 1700: Kangxi Porcelains at the Taft Museum,* Sept. 8, 1988–Sept. 17, 1989 (cat. by Sheila Keppel, no. 72).

Literature John Getz, *Catalogue of Chinese Art Objects: Edward R. Bacon Collection,* New York, 1919, p. 11, no. 25, pl. 3; *Catalogue of the Taft Museum,* Cincinnati, 1939 and 1958, no. 468.

1931.142

Rouleau Vase

Kangxi reign (Qing dynasty), ca. 1700
Porcelain, H. 46.3 cm (18¼ in.)
Mark: underglaze blue double ring

This famille verte rouleau vase, enameled in colors and gilt, is decorated with panels depicting the Three Star Gods of Daoism,

1931.161 Lu Xing, with boy attendant

1931.161 Fu Xing, with boy attendant

each identified by a large character on the cylindrical neck: *shou* (longevity) above Shoulao, or Shou Xing, wearing a yellow robe with *shou* in seal characters, grasping his staff, and accompanied by a small boy holding the peach of immortality; *lu* (rank and emolument) above the scholar-official Lu Xing holding his ivory scepter and a boy attendant holding a scroll; *fu* (happiness) above the god Fu Xing holding a long *ruyi* and standing beside bamboo fencing, and a small boy with his arms outstretched. The panels are set on seeded green grounds with loose flowering peony scrolls. The sloping shoulder is decorated with lobed panels representing the Four Liberal Accomplishments, whose attributes include chessboards, books, musical instruments, and scrolls, on flowered trellis- and rosette-pattern grounds.

See 1931.82 (p. 632) for another example of this popular rebus, *Fu-lu-shou san-shing*, incorporating representations of the Three Star Gods of Daoism.

Provenance [Duveen, New York]; Taft collection, Apr. 28, 1902.

Literature John Getz, *A Catalogue of Chinese Porcelains Collected by Mr. and Mrs. Charles P. Taft*, New York, 1904, no. 64; *Catalogue of the Taft Museum*, Cincinnati, 1939 and 1958, no. 467.

1931.161

Rouleau Vase

Kangxi reign (Qing dynasty), ca. 1700
Porcelain, H. 44.4 cm (17½ in.)
Unmarked

This famille verte rouleau vase is enameled in colors and gilt with two large panels: one of six men planting rice in a riverside paddy with a split bamboo bridge spanning the river and a farmhouse among willow trees on the far bank; the other of five women bringing baskets of mulberry leaves as food for stacked trays of silkworms in a riverside house among flowering trees and bamboo. Both panels are inscribed and are framed in black-and-green key fret on seeded green grounds with four *guilong*, or serpentine dragons, among formal flowering lotus. The cylindrical neck is decorated with alternate panels of archaic bronze ritual vessels and flowering branches of day lily and chrysanthemum on flowered cell-pattern grounds.

Sheila Keppel has written that the Kangxi emperor used the theme of sericulture and rice production as a form of imperial propaganda, appropriating the traditional Chinese symbols of peace to reinforce the fact that the residual hostilities between Ming dynasty loyalists and the foreign Manchu rule of the Qing dynasty had ceased nearly twenty years earlier.[1] Known as the "two great foundations of the

1931.162 men planting rice

Fig. 1 Rouleau Vase and *Peiwen Zhai Gengzhi Tu,* or *Peiwen* Studio Pictures of Plowing and Weaving. Woodblock-printed book, Japanese reprint of late nineteenth century after original from reign of the Qianlong emperor, 1736–95. Book: collection of Dr. James Cahill, Berkeley, Calif.

empire," silkworm culture and rice planting had been initiated each spring for four thousand years by the empress and emperor with elaborate personal rituals. By assuming that traditional role, the Kangxi emperor clearly illustrated the development of the Qing dynasty from its nomadic Manchu origin to a stable, agricultural Chinese society.

The Kangxi emperor commissioned a series of paintings of plowing and weaving from the court painter Jiao Bingzhen, based on the original manuscript by Lou Shou published in 1145 (the text is now lost although subsequent printings exist). In 1696, also at the emperor's command, these paintings were issued as a wood-block–printed book, cut by Zhu Gui and accompanied by descriptive poems ascribed to the Kangxi emperor: *Yuzhi Gengzhi Tu,* or *By Imperial Command: Pictures of Plowing and Weaving.* In his introduction to *By Imperial Command,* the emperor emphatically declared his appreciation of the agricultural workers in China, while subtly asserting the legitimacy of his Manchu reign: "I also ordered engraved plates to be made based on the pictures . . . in order to show them to later generations of the imperial house, and to officials and commoners as well. The pictures will enable them to realize that every grain and every piece of cloth are products of toiling."[2]

During the seventeenth century, wood-block images were already well established as source models for the decoration of ceramics dating from the Transitional Period. The plowing and weaving pictures were quickly translated to porcelain in the later years of the Kangxi reign and continued to be used during the reigns of the Yongzheng (1723–35) and Qianlong (1736–95) emperors. As Keppel stated, "The fact that these porcelains were designed so promptly after publishing, with an almost unprecedented degree of faithfulness to the printed models, points to a direct propaganda effort on the part of the Kangxi Emperor."[3]

The two compositions on this vase are each accompanied by the forty-character poem believed to have been written by the emperor. On one side appears the "Second Transplanting," which occurs after the rice grains have been sprouted in water and subsequently plowed and harrowed. In the upper right of the composition appears the emperor's poem:

> At early morn we begin our work.
> The plants must be sown in straight lines and evenly apart.
> With the bundle on the left arm we plant on the right.
> Beginning from the left each his line toward the right.
> Amidst song and talk thus we pass the day.
> This is the husbandmen's busiest of times.[4]

On the opposite side the poem describes the feeding of silkworm larvae:

> The leaves are brought in baskets.
> The noise of eating is like the dropping of rain.
> Our womenkind are now at their busiest.
> Ah! those who flaunt their silks and satins,
> Little know they of the labor of their country friends.[5]

1. Sheila Keppel, *China in 1700: Kangxi Porcelains at the Taft Museum,* exh. cat., Cincinnati, 1988, p. 10.

2. *Yuzhi Gengzhi Tu,* Shanghai, reprint 1879, n.p., translations in English and French by the editor.

3. Keppel, p. 10.

4. *Yuzhi Gengzhi Tu,* n.p.
5. *Yuzhi Gengzhi Tu,* n.p.

Provenance [Duveen, New York]; Taft collection, Apr. 28, 1902.

Exhibition Cincinnati, Taft Museum [also Flint, Mich., and Muncie, Ind.], *China in 1700: Kangxi Porcelains at the Taft Museum,* Sept. 8, 1988–Sept. 17, 1989 (cat. by Sheila Keppel, no. 32).

Literature John Getz, *A Catalogue of Chinese Porcelains Collected by Mr. and Mrs. Charles P. Taft,* New York, 1904, no. 65; *Catalogue of the Taft Museum,* Cincinnati, 1939 and 1958, no. 456.

1931.162

Rouleau Vase

Kangxi reign (Qing dynasty), ca. 1700
Porcelain, H. 45.7 cm (18 in.)
Mark: underglaze blue double ring

This famille verte rouleau vase, enameled in colors and gilt, depicts a high civil official seated in a canopied tumbril being escorted by foot and cavalry soldiers through a cloudy mountain pass. The rounded shoulder is decorated with trailing clouds below blue enamel *shou* characters, the symbol for long life, placed low on the neck.

The scene on this vase may be identified as Kung Ming (formally referred to as Zhu Ge Liang), seated in the tumbril, and the following line from the *Sanguozhi Yanyi,* or *The Romance of the Three Kingdoms:* "Now the sword and the spear are all around us."[1] Presumably written in its current form by the fourteenth-century author Luo Guanzhong (ca. 1330–ca. 1400), *The Romance of the Three Kingdoms* is a novel based on an official work of history by Chen Shou (233–297).[2] A sprawling narrative of human ambition, the novel is a compilation of historical events and characters with fictional anecdotes added. During the Yuan dynasty (1271–1368), when this work was probably written, China was under the foreign rule of the Mongols, who occupied and exploited the country. Little documentation survives about Luo Guanzhong except that his writing indicates that he was trained and educated as a member of the scholar-official class that ruled China, although he did not hold a post in that government.[3]

Based on events occurring during the third century A.D. when the Han dynasty (206 B.C.–A.D. 220) empire disintegrated and China was splintered into the Three Kingdoms (A.D. 220–65), *The Romance of the Three Kingdoms* chronicles the efforts of Liu Bei, a member of the Han imperial family, to reunite his country. With his base of power in Sichuan, known as the Kingdom of Shu, Liu Bei formed an alliance with Guan Yu (see 1931.33, p. 615), a member of the literati, or scholar-gentry, and Chang Fei, a commoner who had earned his living as a butcher, to wage war against Cao Cao, the ruler of the Kingdom of Wei, who had seized control of North China around 219. With the advice of Zhu Ge Liang (181–234),[4] a master military and political strategist, the trio of heroic patriots fought for many years against Cao Cao's army of mercenaries and nomadic herdsmen but was un-

1931.159 Kung Ming in tumbril

1931.159 lantern and standard bearers

successful in either overthrowing the Wei leader or conquering the Kingdom of Wu, which was based at Nanking.

The figures on the Taft vase are portrayed in contemporary early-eighteenth-century attire rather than in historical costumes, suggesting that this decorative scheme was based on one of the more than one hundred dramas drawn from the fourteenth-century source in later periods.[5] Scenes from this epic also appear on two other rouleau vases in the Taft collection (see 1931.140 and 146, pp. 642–43), dated to the reign of the Kangxi emperor. This patriotic theme may have been resurrected at this time as a subtle form of imperial propaganda, emphasizing loyalty to a new unified China under the Manchu rule of the Qing dynasty. The use of this novel as political propaganda during the reign of the Kangxi emperor intentionally draws a parallel between the exploitation of the Chinese peasant class and the natural resources of the countryside by the Mongols of the Yuan dynasty and the corruption of the government of the Ming dynasty. The Kangxi emperor masterfully appropriated themes from China's past to validate his own foreign Manchu rule as a just and legitimate alternative to that of the Ming dynasty.

1. Sheila Keppel, *China in 1700: Kangxi Porcelains at the Taft Museum*, exh. cat., Cincinnati, 1988, p. 12.

2. Luo Guanzhong, *The Romance of the Three Kingdoms*, trans. C. H. Brewitt-Taylor, vol. 1, Tokyo, 1990, p. vi.

3. Luo Guanzhong, p. viii.

4. Jacques Gernet, *A History of Chinese Civilization*, trans. J. R. Forster, Cambridge, 1990, p. 178.

5. Keppel, p. 12.

Provenance [Duveen, New York]; Taft collection, May 22, 1903.

Exhibition Cincinnati, Taft Museum [also Flint, Mich., and Muncie, Ind.], *China in 1700: Kangxi Porcelains at the Taft Museum*, Sept. 8, 1988–Sept. 17, 1989 (cat. by Sheila Keppel, no. 46).

Literature John Getz, *A Catalogue of Chinese Porcelains Collected by Mr. and Mrs. Charles P. Taft*, New York, 1904, no. 63; *Catalogue of the Taft Museum*, Cincinnati, 1939 and 1958, no. 457.

1931.159

Rouleau Vase

Kangxi reign (Qing dynasty), ca. 1700
Porcelain, H. 45.7 cm (18 in.)
Mark: underglaze blue artemisia leaf within double ring

This famille verte rouleau vase is enameled in colors and gilt with eleven rectangular panels showing scenes from popular romances on a seeded green ground scattered with prunus blossoms and white cranes. The sloping shoulder is decorated with a band of *ruyi* lappets; the trumpet neck, with fan-shaped landscape panels; and the thumb-indented lip, with a green hatched pattern.

The subject illustrated on this vase is derived from the fourteenth-century novel *Xi Xiang Ji*, or *The Romance of the Western Chamber*,[1] written by Wang Shifu during the Yuan dynasty

1931.164 Zhang Junrui meeting the maid Hongniang

(1279–1368). *Xi Xiang Ji* is a composite of five connected *zaju*, or dramas, based on *Yingying Zhuan*, or *The Biography of Cui Yingying*, a Tang dynasty story by Yuan Zhen (799–831), with expanded story line and songs added by Dong Jieyuan during the reign of the Zhangzong emperor (1190–1209) in the Jin dynasty.[2] Widely published as wood-block illustrations beginning in the fourteenth century and reaching its greatest popularity during the reign of the Kangxi emperor, this narrative's longevity as a source of ceramic decoration has been attributed by Stephen Little to its lack of direct political content.[3]

The scenes on this vase focus on the love affair between the heroine Cui Yingying and Zhang Junrui, a scholar who is preparing for the upcoming civil-service examinations. In 801 Yingying, her mother, and ladies' maid, Hongniang, stop at the Buddhist monastery Pu Jiu while making a journey to bury Madame Zheng's late husband, the former prime minister.

Zhang Junrui glimpses the beautiful but cold heroine while visiting the monastery and secures a room there in hopes of becoming acquainted with her. Meanwhile, Sun, the Flying Tiger, a rogue soldier who commands five thousand bandit troops, hears of Yingying's beauty and decides to capture her affections forcibly. With Sun's troops surrounding the monastery, Madame Zheng offers her daughter as wife to any man who can drive off the bandit. Zhang Junrui writes to a childhood friend General

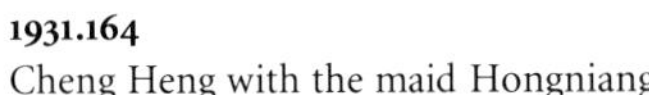

1931.164
Cheng Heng with the maid Hongniang

1931.164
Zhang Junrui confronting Sun

1931.164
woman meeting with official

Du Jue, who commands one hundred thousand troops, asking that he send soldiers to liberate the monastery. The bandit's troops are defeated and Sun is beheaded, but Madame Zheng refuses to honor her promise to Zhang Junrui, noting that Yingying is already engaged to Madame Zheng's nephew.

Yingying and Zhang Junrui arrange a rendezvous in the gardens at night and fall in love. After Yingying's mother extracts the details of the lovers' secret meeting from the servant, Hongniang, who has encouraged the affair, she agrees to accept Zhang Junrui as her son-in-law, but only after he passes the civil-service examinations in the capital city of Chang'an. Nearly six months later, Zhang Junrui sends a triumphant message to Yingying that he has placed third in the examinations and is about to receive notice of an official post. Finally, he and Yingying are reunited at the monastery, and Madame Zheng gives permission for them to marry honorably.[4]

In some versions of the novel and in some of the many dramas drawn from it, Yingying dies before Zhang Junrui can return from Chang'an with news of his post. Another porcelain vase in the Taft collection depicts Yingying rising from her grave to join Zhang Junrui in the Peony Pavilion (see 1931.176, p. 656),[5] while a charger depicts "The Interruption of the Religious Service" (1931.185, p. 675).

Among the identifiable vignettes on the Taft vase are scenes of the maid watching as a seated Yingying reads a letter from Zhang Junrui announcing that he has passed the examinations (lower register), and the young scholar in battle with Sun, the Flying Tiger (central register).

Possible interpretations of the remaining scenes include, in the top register — Zhang Junrui meeting with the maid to declare his love for Yingying; Cheng Heng, Madame Zheng's nephew, to whom Yingying is betrothed, informing the maid that he has come to the monastery to claim Yingying; and an unidentified scene of three women having an audience with an official; in the middle register — an unidentified woman meeting with an official; and Zhang Junrui giving a letter to a servant from the monastery, probably for delivery to the general who defeats Sun; and in the lower register — a female Daoist Immortal (perhaps Lan Caihe, patron of gardeners: see 1931.42, p. 618) with an unidentified male Immortal; and Zhang Junrui receiving a sword from two men.

The story, however, is not illustrated as a complete narrative, as Keppel documents. Painters of ceramic decorations drew their inspiration from *fenben*, or sketches such as wood-block illustrations, which were accumulated and reused over many years, often being combined in random order, as on this example.[6]

The combination of prunus blossoms (which in China are equated with beauty and fortune), white cranes (symbolic of longevity), and the *ruyi* decoration represents a wish-fulfilling rebus for long life and good fortune — a visual pun appropriate to the romantic subject matter depicted on the panels.

1. Sheila Keppel, *China in 1700: Kangxi Porcelains at the Taft Museum*, exh. cat., Cincinnati, 1988, p. 12.

2. Craig Clunas, "The Western Chamber: A Literary Theme in Chinese Porcelain Decoration," *Transactions of the Oriental Ceramic Society*, vol. XLVI (1981–82), p. 69.

3. Stephen Little, "Narrative Themes and Woodblock Prints in the Decoration of Seventeenth-Century Chinese Porcelains," *Seventeenth-Century Chinese Porcelain from the Butler Family Collection,* exh. cat., Art Services International, Alexandria, Va., 1990, p. 27.

4. S. I. Hsiung, trans., *The Romance of the Western Chamber,* New York, 1936.

5. Keppel, p. 12.

6. Keppel, p. 12.

Provenance [Duveen, New York]; Taft collection, Apr. 28, 1902.

Exhibition Cincinnati, Taft Museum [also Flint, Mich., and Muncie, Ind.], *China in 1700: Kangxi Porcelains at the Taft Museum,* Sept. 8, 1988–Sept. 17, 1989 (cat. by Sheila Keppel, no. 44).

Literature John Getz, *A Catalogue of Chinese Porcelains Collected by Mr. and Mrs. Charles P. Taft,* New York, 1904, no. 66; *Catalogue of the Taft Museum,* Cincinnati, 1939 and 1958, no. 547.

1931.164

Pair of Rouleau Vases

Kangxi reign (Qing dynasty), early eighteenth century
Porcelain: 1931.140, H. 73 cm (28¾ in.); 1931.146, H. 73.7 cm (29 in.)
Unmarked

Each of this pair of massive famille verte rouleau vases is modeled and carved in high relief on the sides and neck and enameled in colors and gilt. The scenes on both vases depict Hiding the Baby among the Ten Thousand Soldiers, a famous battle that occurred at Changbanpo, from the fourteenth-century epic drama *Sanguozhi Yanyi,* or *The Romance of the Three Kingdoms.*

On one vase (1931.140) five soldiers — two with snares and three with swords, halberds, and maces — attack Zhao Yun, who has the infant son of Liu Bei strapped to his waist and a dream cloud containing a *mang,* or horned four-clawed dragon, issuing from his back. On the other side of the vase, separated from the action below by an edge of the dream cloud, are two official personages, perhaps Liu Bei and his wife, with an attendant, all standing beneath a banner with the *ling* symbol of a commanding officer. Behind them on a stone bridge are a mounted warrior, perhaps Guan Yu, and an attendant, both armed; below are two mounted, armed soldiers and the leader of the warriors attacking Zhao Yun.

On the other vase (1931.146), a small demon brandishes two clubs and releases from the bottle gourd at his neck a dream cloud of blackbirds that attacks a fierce red-headed man or Daoist demon mounted on a lion and commanding two wolves, a leopard, and a tiger. Holding this figure and his creatures at bay are two flanking lines of mounted halberdiers, while above Zhao Yun escapes with his commander's infant son under a banner bearing the *yin yang* symbol, representing the positive and negative principles of universal life.

The bases of both vases are decorated with spiraling petals; the sloping shoulders with panels of flowering and fruiting quince, peach, pomegranate, Buddha-hand citron, and lotus on iron red and gilt chrysanthemum scroll grounds. The necks are

1931.140 Zhao Yun on horseback

1931.146 demon brandishing clubs

1931.140 two official personages

1931.140 mounted warrior on bridge (above)

1931.146 Zhao Yun escaping with Liu Bei's son

1931.146 Zhao Yun's troops

decorated with two horned gilt and enameled dragons chasing flaming pearls — one vase with two four-clawed dragons and the other vase with two three-clawed dragons. The recessed bands above the sloping shoulders are decorated with formal patterned band borders.

In *The Romance of the Three Kingdoms,* as well as in the more than one hundred plays derived from it, Zhao Yun rescues the son of Liu Bei, a member of the Han dynasty (206 B.C.–A.D. 220) imperial family who joined forces with Guan Yu and Chang Fei in an attempt to reunite their splintered country (see 1931.159, p. 639). Many historical battles, such as the one at Changbanpo depicted on this pair of vases, were later believed to have been won with the intervention of Daoist supernatural forces. On 1931.146, for example, the mounted halberdier carrying a banner with the *yin yang* symbol on it and the small demon or Immortal releasing spirits in the form of blackbirds from the bottle gourd at his neck refer to magical Daoist assistance, even though Daoism was not widespread in China during the Han dynasty.

Provenance [Duveen, New York (as late Kangxi)]; Taft collection, Apr. 13, 1904.

Literature John Getz, *A Catalogue of Chinese Porcelains Collected by Mr. and Mrs. Charles P. Taft,* New York, 1904, nos. 71–72; *Catalogue of the Taft Museum,* Cincinnati, 1939 and 1958, nos. 1, 8.

1931.140, 1931.146

1931.160 Lin Xiu in armor and Deng Yu in scholar's attire

Rouleau Vase

Kangxi reign (Qing dynasty), ca. 1700–1722
Porcelain, H. 75 cm (29½ in.)
Mark: underglaze blue double ring

This massive famille verte rouleau vase is enameled in colors and gilt on the body with an elaborate battle scene. A general looks from a battlemented gatehouse as mounted retainers surge through it toward figures mounted on and surrounded by fanciful animals. The shoulder is decorated with panels depicting scholar's objects on a green-and-black enamel brocade ground, and the cylindrical neck is enameled with rectangular landscape panels divided by iron red and gilt archaic *guilong,* or serpentine dragons, holding branches of *lingzhi,* all below bands of lappets and a green key pattern on the short straight lip.

The battle scene on this vase depicts *The Tale of Kunyang City,* a historical event concerning the fall from power of the usurper Wang Meng. Meng had seized control of China after the fall of the Western Han dynasty in about 6 A.D. The lengthy Han dynasty was divided into two periods, the Western Han (206 B.C.–A.D. 8) and the Eastern Han (A.D. 25–220), by the short, chaotic rule of Wang Meng's new Xin dynasty (A.D. 9–23). He unsuccessfully attempted to institute a series of radical reforms, including nationalizing vast landholdings and implementing a new monetary system, which led to widespread revolts.[1] These uprisings, instituted by peasants and members of the Han nobility who painted their faces to represent demons and called themselves the *chi-mei,* or "Red Eyebrows," resulted in the restoration of the Han dynasty. After the defeat and death of Wang Meng, China was unified and stabilized under the rule of Lin Xiu, who ruled under the name of Guang Wudi (A.D. 25–57).[2]

Identifying the subject of the scene, the characters over the city gate read "Kunyang City." The two figures standing on the city wall above the gate and discussing battle strategies are Lin Xiu in armor and wearing a helmet, a descendant of the Western Han royal house who was placed on a throne rivaling Wang Meng's, and his general, Deng Yu, in scholar's attire. To the left of the city wall, riding a lion and holding a sword and shield, is Wang Meng's general, Wang Xin, who was dispatched at the head of extensive troops to recapture Kunyang from Lin Xiu's control. Lin Xiu appears again, ready to impale Wang Xin with a lance as he charges out of the city on horseback, leading a small suicide squad under a general's banner against the enemy. At the forefront of the charge is a figure with a bottle gourd on his back who probably represents a Daoist Immortal or demon calling forth a violent rainstorm to terrify Wang Xin's army of soldiers and wild beasts. This action suggests that magical Daoist forces aided Lin Xiu in defeating an overwhelming enemy.[3]

Sheila Keppel has written of this scene, "The figural design and painting show considerable sophistication, . . . probably indicating the style of a very competent court painter, Liu Yuan, who provided Jingdezhen with 'hundreds of designs of figures, flowers, and landscapes' between 1682 and c. 1688."[4]

1. Jacques Gernet, *A History of Chinese Civilization,* trans. J. R. Foster, Cambridge, 1990, pp. 149–50.

1931.160 Lin Xiu about to impale Wang Xin

2. Gernet, pp. 150–51.

3. Identification of subject taken from correspondence with National Palace Museum, Taipei, Taiwan, June 3, 1970 (Taft Museum archives).

4. Sheila Keppel, *China in 1700: Kangxi Porcelains at the Taft Museum*, exh. cat., Cincinnati, 1988, p. 12.

Provenance Errazzu collection (according to Duveen invoice); [Duveen, New York]; Taft collection, Mar. 28, 1908.

Exhibition Cincinnati, Taft Museum [also Flint, Mich., and Muncie, Ind.], *China in 1700: Kangxi Porcelains at the Taft Museum*, Sept. 8, 1988–Sept. 17, 1989 (cat. by Sheila Keppel, no. 45).

Literature *Catalogue of the Taft Museum*, Cincinnati, 1939 and 1958, no. 229.

1931.160

Baluster Vase

Kangxi reign (Qing dynasty), 1662–1722
Porcelain, H. 76.2 cm (30 in.)
Unmarked

This famille verte tall baluster vase with trumpet neck is enameled in colors and gilt with elaborately shaped panels of landscapes, mythical beasts, cranes among lotus, pheasants, and small birds on flowering branches, all on green shagreen grounds scattered with formal chrysanthemum heads, palm

1931.160 Wang Xin riding a lion

1931.139

1931.139

leaves, and *babao,* or Eight Precious Things. The base, shoulder, and lip are decorated with bands of musical instruments, Buddhistic lions, and *babao* on various brocade-pattern grounds.

Provenance George Salting, London (according to Duveen invoice); [Duveen, New York]; Taft collection, Oct. 21, 1902.

Exhibition Cincinnati, Taft Museum [also Flint, Mich., and Muncie, Ind.], *China in 1700: Kangxi Porcelains at the Taft Museum,* Sept. 8, 1988–Sept. 17, 1989 (cat. by Sheila Keppel, no. 26).

Literature John Getz, *A Catalogue of Chinese Porcelains Collected by Mr. and Mrs. Charles P. Taft,* New York, 1904, no. 62; *Catalogue of the Taft Museum,* Cincinnati, 1939 and 1958, no. 208.

1931.139

Baluster Vases with Table Stands and Domed Covers

Kangxi reign (Qing dynasty), ca. 1680–1700
Porcelain, H. 26 cm (10¼ in.)
Unmarked

This pair of famille verte octagonal baluster vases with table stands and domed covers is enameled on the biscuit in greens, yellow, black, and aubergine. The vases are decorated with quatrefoil panels of formal lotus on trellis-patterned grounds above

1931.17, 19

bands of overlapping leaves and below relief-molded lotus petals on the shoulders and covers. Around the bases are green-ground classical scroll bands. The finials are squared knobs, and the flowered stands rest on quatrefoil bases.

Provenance Blenheim Palace (sale, Christie's, London, Aug. 3, 1886, no. 402, £51.9s); James A. Garland, New York (in 1895); [Duveen, New York]; Taft collection, Oct. 21, 1902.

Exhibition New York, The Metropolitan Museum of Art, 1895 (*Handbook of a Collection of Chinese Porcelains Loaned by James A. Garland,* cat. by John Getz, p. 46b, ill. "Case 14").

Literature John Getz, *A Catalogue of Chinese Porcelains Collected by Mr. and Mrs. Charles P. Taft,* New York, 1904, no. 54; *Catalogue of the Taft Museum,* Cincinnati, 1939 and 1958, nos. 297, 299.

1931.17, 1931.19

Workshop of Edmé Samson (1810–1891)

Pair of Baluster Vases

French, late nineteenth century
Porcelain, H. 22.5 cm (8⅞ in.)
Unmarked

This pair of slender hexagonal baluster vases is enameled in the famille verte style with the *babao,* or Eight Precious Things, scattered among flower heads on green breaking waves.

The vases were made by Edmé Samson in Montreuil as forgeries of famille verte originals from the Kangxi period. Samson was a French nineteenth-century artist specializing in romantic scenes, who established a factory outside Paris that first copied

1931.39, 43

1931.47

and later made deceptive reproductions of porcelains in all styles, especially Meissen, Sèvres, Chelsea, and Chinese export wares. Samson's son, Emile (1837–1913), and his successive generations continued to direct the factory, producing reproductions of enamels, gilt bronzes, and ceramics.

Samson's forgeries of Chinese porcelains can usually be recognized by their white crystalline bodies with blue pooling in the glaze. The painting is much stiffer than and lacks the freedom of the typical Kangxi-period export wares.

Provenance S. E. Kennedy; [Parish-Watson, New York]; Taft collection, Oct. 30, 1924.

Literature *Catalogue of the Taft Museum,* Cincinnati, 1939 and 1958, nos. 286, 288.

1931.39, 1931.43

Arrow Vase

Kangxi reign (Qing dynasty), ca. 1700
Porcelain with gilt-bronze mounts (French, ca. 1740),
H. 37 cm (14½ in.)
Unmarked

This famille verte hollow square vase consists of a three-part section mounted on a stepped gilt-bronze base cast with overlapping leaves. The porcelain is molded with panels of *shou,* the symbol of longevity, surrounded by archaic *guilong,* or serpentine dragons, and is decorated with applied porcelain panels set within peach branches at the top. The center is enameled in colors with a band of horned *guilong* among lotus. The lower part has four-clawed *mang* dragons grasping sacred pearls within cloud and flame roundels.

This arrow vase may have originally had tubular "ears," as the Chinese refer to such handles, where the applied rectangular floral slabs are now attached. Arrows were kept in the ears of the vessel for pitchpot, a game of dexterity in which arrows were thrown from a distance into the mouth of the pot or, most skillfully, into the ears. Derived from Manchu nomadic origins, the rectangular shape of the Taft arrow vase may have been introduced during the seventeenth century. Vessels with pierced ears, in imitation of bronze *touhu* and associated with the game of pitchpot, nevertheless have been in the Chinese ceramic vocabulary since the Southern Song dynasty (1127–1279).[1]

The slab panels among the peaches are clearly period, but from another object. The plaster branches joined to the original peaches (one on each side is plaster) are possibly additions from the time of the mounting. The original porcelain base has been replaced with gilt-bronze French mounts.

1. See René-Yvon Lefebvre d'Argencé, ed., *Treasures from the Shanghai Museum: Six Thousand Years of Chinese Art,* exh. cat., Shanghai Museum and Asian Art Museum of San Francisco, 1983, p. 162, no. 82, for a rare example of a porcelaneous *ge*-ware vase with pierced ears (ill. p. 101).

Provenance [Duveen, New York]; Taft collection, Oct. 21, 1902.

Exhibition Cincinnati, Taft Museum [also Flint, Mich., and Muncie, Ind.], *China in 1700: Kangxi Porcelains at the Taft Museum,* Sept. 8, 1988–Sept. 17, 1989 (cat. by Sheila Keppel, no. 25).

Literature John Getz, *A Catalogue of Chinese Porcelains Collected by Mr. and Mrs. Charles P. Taft*, New York, 1904, no. 70; *Catalogue of the Taft Museum*, Cincinnati, 1939 and 1958, no. 309.

1931.47

Square Tapering Vase

Kangxi reign (Qing dynasty), ca. 1700
Porcelain with gilt-bronze mounts (French, eighteenth century), H. 44.8 cm (17⅝ in.)
Unmarked

This famille verte square tapering vase with trumpet neck and flared base is decorated on each side with enameled and gilded high-relief molded figures: Shou Xing, or Shoulao, god of longevity, grasping his staff, and his boy attendant, holding a long-stemmed *ruyi*, under a pine tree with an inscription in archaic Chinese above; Lu Xing, god of rank and emolument, also with a boy attendant, holding a long-stemmed lotus flower, and a similar inscription above; Fu Xing, god of blessings, holding a *ruyi* scepter and accompanied by a boy attendant who carries a vase containing a halberd and *qing*, or stone chime; and Zhang Xian, known as the purveyor of children, with a boy attendant, holding a *sheng*, or reed flute. Zhang Xian, the patron of child-bearing women, is always accompanied by one or more small boys.[1] On this vase, he holds a bow, having just shot an arrow at the Heavenly Dog, also known as the Child-Stealing Devil, a celestial star that is a bad omen since it shortens the life spans of children. The Chinese believe that this star is the spirit of a woman who died unmarried and seeks offspring by killing chil-

1931.92 Zhang Xian

1931.92 Shou Xing

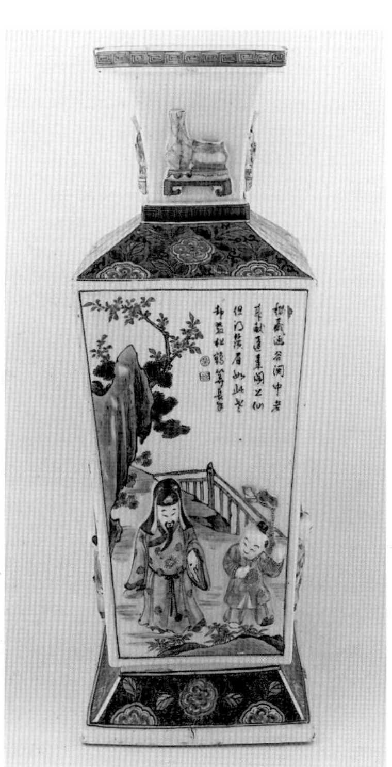

1931.92 Lu Xing

1931.92 Fu Xing

dren.[2] The flaring base and sloping shoulder are enameled with formal flowering branches on seeded grounds. The trumpet neck is decorated with vases and burners on low tables in high relief. The rim is decorated with a green key pattern, symbolic of rebirth, and the vase has been mounted at a later date on a square French ormolu base chased with a band of stiff leaves.[3]

The combination of the Three Star Gods of Daoism with Zhang Xian forms a series of complex rebuses that express the wish for the birth of a male heir who will increase the family's prestige and wealth by entering the Chinese civil service. Shou Xing's attendant carries a *ruyi,* the most auspicious Chinese symbol, which means "as you wish." Lu Xing's attendant carries a lotus, symbolizing marriage. Zhang Xian's attendant carries a *sheng,* homophonous for "to give birth." Fu Xing's attendant carries a vase holding a halberd, symbolic of luck, with a stone chime hanging from it: vase, or *ping,* shares the same sound as "peace," and halberd, or *ji,* is homophonous with "step" and "rank." The resulting rebus, *pingsheng ji,* or "may you rise a step in rapid succession," is a wish for the boy's success in the civil service.[4] The stone chime, or *qing,* is symbolic of joy and celebration, as would occur if the child fared well in his bureaucratic career.

1. Tseng Yu-ho Ecke, *Chinese Folk Art II,* Honolulu, 1977, p. 103. I am grateful to Terese Tse Bartholomew, curator of Indian and Himalayan Art, Asian Art Museum of San Francisco, for identifying this rebus.

2. C. A. S. Williams, *Outlines of Chinese Symbolism and Art Motives,* New York, 1977, p. 62.

3. See John Getz, *Catalogue of Chinese Art Objects: Edward R. Bacon Collection,* New York, 1919, p. 26, no. 54, pl. x, and Alphonse Favier, *Peking: Histoire et description,* Peking, 1897, pl. xxxvi, for comparative examples.

4. Terese Tse Bartholomew, *Myths and Rebuses in Chinese Art,* exh. cat., Asian Art Museum of San Francisco, 1988, n.p.

Provenance [Duveen, New York]; Taft collection, June 14, 1902.

Literature John Getz, *A Catalogue of Chinese Porcelains Collected by Mr. and Mrs. Charles P. Taft,* New York, 1904, no. 69; *Catalogue of the Taft Museum,* Cincinnati, 1939 and 1958, no. 311.

1931.92

Square Tapering Vase

Kangxi reign (Qing dynasty), ca. 1700–1722
Porcelain, H. 47 cm (18½ in.)
Unmarked

The sides of this famille verte square tapering vase with trumpet neck and stepped base have applied high-relief shaped panels of birds, mythical beasts, landscapes, and flowering branches on grounds enameled with formal chrysanthemum branches on a black-and-green whorl pattern within hatched borders. The sloping shoulder is decorated with raised *ruyi* lappets and key pattern below green stiff leaves on the neck and clouds on the everted lip.

Provenance [Duveen, New York]; Taft collection, June 14, 1902.

1931.94

Literature John Getz, *A Catalogue of Chinese Porcelains Collected by Mr. and Mrs. Charles P. Taft,* New York, 1904, no. 68; *Catalogue of the Taft Museum,* Cincinnati, 1939 and 1958, no. 546.

1931.94

Square Tapering Vase

Qing dynasty, nineteenth century
Porcelain, H. 52 cm (19¾ in.)
Mark: dedicatory underglaze blue six-character Chenghua reign mark (1456–87); not of the period

This square tapering vase with trumpet neck is enameled in the famille verte palette. Two sides with green grounds show pheasants and small birds among flowering branches of prunus, peony, and magnolia. The other two sides have white grounds, one with Shoulao on a terrace presenting a peach to Fu Xing and Lu Xing, accompanied by boy attendants, standing under a pine tree, and the other with Xi Wangmu, Queen Mother of the West, riding a phoenix, watched by Shoulao and the Eight Daoist Immortals standing on rocky ledges by a lake. The trum-

1931.155 Shoulao offering Peach of Immortality to Lu Xing and Fu Xing

1931.155 detail of birds among prunus

1931.155 Xi Wangmu riding a phoenix and Shoulao holding a peach branch

pet neck is decorated with a panel of Shoulao holding a peach branch and a four-line poem.

S. Lockhart has translated the poem on the neck: "In the morning its beauty widely spreads the dew of fairy hands; at night its fragrance intensely attracts the wind of the Jade-stone hall."[1] This verse refers to the reputation of the Hanlin *Yuan,* or academy, an official bureau in China during the Ming dynasty composed of scholars who achieved the highest literary degrees.[2]

1. In John Getz, *A Catalogue of Chinese Porcelains Collected by Mr. and Mrs. Charles P. Taft,* New York, 1904, p. 96.

2. Terese Tse Bartholomew, *Myths and Rebuses in Chinese Art,* exh. cat., Asian Art Museum of San Francisco, 1988, n.p.

1931.155 detail of mark

Provenance [Duveen, New York]; Taft collection, Apr. 28, 1902.

Literature John Getz, *A Catalogue of Chinese Porcelains Collected by Mr. and Mrs. Charles P. Taft,* New York, 1904, no. 73; *Catalogue of the Taft Museum,* Cincinnati, 1939 and 1958, no. 435.

1931.155

Two Bottle Vases

Kangxi reign (Qing dynasty), ca. 1700
Porcelain, H. 23.5 cm (9¼ in.)
Mark: underglaze blue script *G*

These two famille verte bottle vases with tall cylindrical necks are each enameled in colors and gilt with an allover pattern of loosely scrolling formal flowering branches, meant to represent chrysanthemums. The shoulders are decorated with bands of formal flowers and foliage scrolls on seeded aubergine grounds, and the necks are enameled with the pattern from the bodies repeated below cell-pattern brocade borders.

The shape of these vases, which are sometimes called point bottles, is derived from early Near Eastern metal and glass rosewater sprinklers. The marks probably refer to one of the Dutch East India companies that may have ordered these vases. Identical marks are known on Chinese export wares, but the script *G* has yet to be firmly documented or traced to a specific trading company.[1]

1931.85 detail of mark

1931.83, 85

1. See John Ayers, *Chinese Ceramics: The Kroger Collection,* London, 1985, p. 142, ill. p. 113, for another example of this shape bearing a script European *G* as a mark.

Provenance [Duveen, New York]; Taft collection, Oct. 21, 1902.

Literature John Getz, *A Catalogue of Chinese Porcelains Collected by Mr. and Mrs. Charles P. Taft,* New York, 1904, nos. 59–60; *Catalogue of the Taft Museum,* Cincinnati, 1939 and 1958, nos. 361, 365.

1931.83, 1931.85

Bamboo Vase with Table Stand

Kangxi reign (Qing dynasty), ca. 1662–75
Porcelain, H. 21.6 cm (8½ in.)
Unmarked

This famille verte bamboo vase is set into a quatrefoil table stand. The body is molded as a cluster of bamboo canes on top of a lotus flower below a quatrefoil trumpet neck with bamboo twig handles. The body and stand are enameled on the biscuit with flowers in light and dark aubergine, green, and yellow; the neck has a trellis- and seed-pattern ground.

1931.74

Provenance James A. Garland, New York (1895–1902); [Duveen, New York (as Ming)]; Taft collection, Nov. 10, 1905.

Exhibition New York, The Metropolitan Museum of Art, 1895 (*Handbook of a Collection of Chinese Porcelain Loaned by James A. Garland,* cat. by John Getz, ill. "Case 14").

Literature *Catalogue of the Taft Museum,* Cincinnati, 1939 and 1958, no. 334.

1931.74

1931.34, 38

Pair of Triple Bottle-Gourd Vases

Kangxi reign (Qing dynasty), ca. 1700
Porcelain, H. 25.4 cm (10 in.)
Mark: underglaze blue double ring

This pair of famille verte triple bottle-gourd vases with everted lips is enameled with bright leaf green grounds reserved in white with formal flowering peony scrolls, outlined in sepia.

Provenance [Parish-Watson, New York]; Taft collection, Apr. 14, 1924.

Literature *Catalogue of the Taft Museum,* Cincinnati, 1939 and 1958, nos. 101, 103.

1931.34, 1931.38

Meiping

Kangxi reign (Qing dynasty), 1662–1722
Porcelain, H. 30.2 cm (11⅞ in.)
Unmarked

This famille verte *meiping* has a slender body with a short trumpet neck and biscuit Buddhistic lion-mask loop handles set low

1931.36

on the sloping shoulders. It is enameled in colors with horned archaic *guilong*, or serpentine dragons, among scrolling flowering lotus on a mottled leaf green ground.

The loop rings for the mask handles are now missing.

Provenance Burghley House, Stamford, Eng. (1886); Louis Huth (sale, Christie's, London, May 17, 1905); Marsden J. Perry; [Duveen, New York]; Taft collection, Mar. 28, 1908.

Literature *Catalogue of the Taft Museum,* Cincinnati, 1939 and 1958, no. 335.

1931.36

Famille Verte with Powder Blue Grounds

Powder blue glazes differ from other Qing blue glazes in that the cobalt was not mixed with the glaze but rather blown onto the vessel through a piece of gauze stretched over the end of a bamboo tube. The ceramic was then covered with a clear glaze and fired. Reserve panels in white containing underglaze blue or overglaze polychrome enamels were often set against powder blue grounds.[1] During the application of the powder blue ground, paper cutouts in the shapes of the reserve panels were attached to the body of the porcelain to shield those areas.

1. Suzanne G. Valenstein, *A Handbook of Chinese Ceramics,* New York, 1989, p. 241.

Teapot with Flat Cover

Kangxi reign (Qing dynasty), ca. 1700
Porcelain, H. 11.5 cm (4½ in.)
Unmarked

This famille verte drum-shaped teapot with flat cover has a plain loop handle and short straight spout. The teapot is enameled in

1931.175

1931.196

colors and gilt with panels of flowering chrysanthemums and pinks growing from rockwork on powder blue grounds with leafy branches, scrolls, and key-fret in gilt. The cover has a lotus bud finial, and nailheads are molded around the top and bottom.

Provenance [Duveen, New York]; Taft collection, Oct. 21, 1902.

Literature John Getz, *A Catalogue of Chinese Porcelains Collected by Mr. and Mrs. Charles P. Taft,* New York, 1904, no. 23; *Catalogue of the Taft Museum,* Cincinnati, 1939 and 1958, no. 47.

1931.175

Circular Charger

Kangxi reign (Qing dynasty), ca. 1700
Porcelain, DIAM. 52.1 cm (20½ in.)
Mark: underglaze blue orchid within double ring

This famille verte circular charger has a central octafoil panel enameled in colors with the Lantern Festival. The scene depicts ladies on the terrace of a pavilion (one playing the *pipa,* or balloon-shaped guitar) looking down at a group of boys. The boys are playing a drum and cymbals as well as holding a pole umbrella and rolling a large brocaded ball toward a suspended carp-dragon lantern surrounded by long tassels. All are being observed by scholars, attendants, and two boys. The iron red octafoil surround is reserved with white flowers and leaf scrolls. The powder blue well has extensive traces of the original gilt decoration of panels of pinks, peonies, poppies, and chrysanthe-

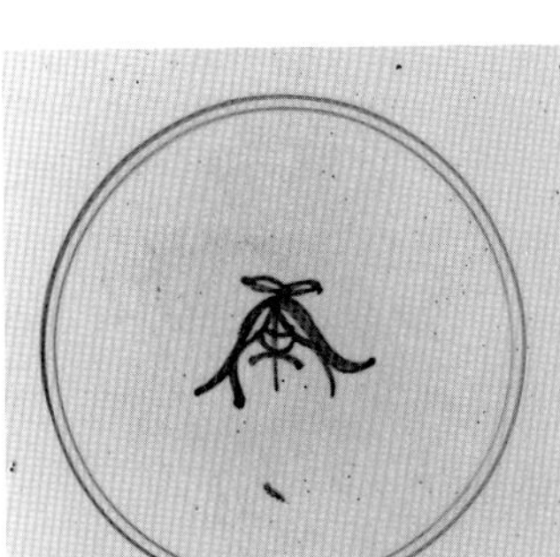

1931.196 detail of mark

mums alternating with the *bogu*, or Hundred Antiques, on a gilt formal ground of lotus and foliage. The reverse is undecorated.

Sheila Keppel has identified the subject of this charger as the capture, at a Lantern Festival, of Song Jiang, the historical outlaw-hero of the fourteenth-century epic novel, *Shuihu Zhuan* (literally *Marsh Chronicles*, but also known as *The Water Margin* or *Outlaws of the Marsh*),[1] written by Shi Nai'an and edited by his student, Luo Guanzhong (the author of *The Romance of the Three Kingdoms*). The action of the novel, which is based on historical fact and folk legend, is primarily set in the final years of Hui Zong, a Song dynasty emperor who reigned from 1101 to 1125. Song Jiang was one of 108 men and women who banded together in the Liangshan marshes (in contemporary Shandong province) to fight against the tyranny of the Song dynasty officials. This group of rebels led an army of thousands in battle against social injustice, their resourceful deeds giving hope to the oppressed Chinese peasants and eventually evolving into folk legends.[2]

By 1642, in the final years of the Ming dynasty (1368–1644), this popular story of widespread peasant uprising was prohibited by imperial decree. The leaders of the Ming insurrections had begun to adopt the names of the outlaw-heroes in *Outlaws of the Marsh* as they rebelled against the oppression of the peasant class by the Ming ruling class, intentionally paralleling the historical subject of the novel.[3] The appearance of a scene from *Outlaws of the Marsh* on a ceramic ware dating from the reign of the Kangxi emperor may be another example of the ruler's program of imperial propaganda, emphasizing loyalty to the new Manchu reign, which liberated peasants by overthrowing the corrupt Ming dynasty.

1. Sheila Keppel, *China in 1700: Kangxi Porcelains at the Taft Museum*, exh. cat., Cincinnati, 1988, p. 13.
2. Shi Nai'an and Luo Guanzhong, *Outlaws of the Marsh*, trans. Sidney Shapiro, 4 vols., Beijing, 1988.
3. Stephen Little, "Narrative Themes and Woodblock Prints in the Decoration of Seventeenth-Century Chinese Porcelains," *Seventeenth-Century Chinese Porcelain from the Butler Family Collection*, exh. cat., Arts Services International, Alexandria, Va., 1990, pp. 25–26.

Provenance [Duveen, New York]; Taft collection, Nov. 10, 1902.

Exhibition Cincinnati, Taft Museum [also Flint, Mich., and Muncie, Ind.], *China in 1700: Kangxi Porcelains at the Taft Museum*, Sept. 8, 1988–Sept. 17, 1989 (cat. by Sheila Keppel, no. 60).

Literature John Getz, *A Catalogue of Chinese Porcelains Collected by Mr. and Mrs. Charles P. Taft*, New York, 1904, no. 29; *Catalogue of the Taft Museum*, Cincinnati, 1939 and 1958, no. 245.

1931.196

Oviform Jar with Domed Cover

Kangxi reign (Qing dynasty), ca. 1700
Porcelain, H. 33 cm (13 in.)
Mark: underglaze blue double ring

1931.171

This famille verte oviform jar with domed cover is enameled in colors and gilt with circular panels of peacocks flying over chrysanthemums, a bird and a duck among lotus and water grasses, and a phoenix flying over peonies. Smaller fan-shaped and square panels illustrate riverscapes and birds and insects among flowering branches. The panels are reserved on a deep powder blue ground and gilded with scattered pine branches, a crab with water grass, and a carp among water weeds above a wide formal lotus scroll at the base, and a band of *ruyi* lappets at the shoulder. The cover is decorated with a circular panel of chrysanthemums growing from rockwork.

Provenance [Duveen, New York]; Taft collection, May 22, 1903.

Literature John Getz, *A Catalogue of Chinese Porcelains Collected by Mr. and Mrs. Charles P. Taft*, New York, 1904, no. 28; *Catalogue of the Taft Museum*, Cincinnati, 1939 and 1958, no. 236.

1931.171

1931.169, 173

1931.169, 173

Pair of Rouleau Vases

Kangxi reign (Qing dynasty), ca. 1700
Porcelain, H. 24.1 cm (9½ in.)
Unmarked

Each of this pair of famille verte rouleau vases is enameled in colors and gilt with two panels of elegant ladies in terraced gardens. On one vase (1931.169) a lady is preening before a mirror set on a rock, and on the reverse another lady is seated holding

1931.169, 173

a fan. On the other vase (1931.173) a lady is standing holding a *lingzhi* scepter; on the reverse another lady is standing holding a fan. The scenes are all on powder blue grounds with gilt classical vases of lotus and chrysanthemum, loose lappet scrolls, and flower sprays.

Provenance [Duveen, New York]; Taft collection, Dec. 12, 1902.
Literature John Getz, *A Catalogue of Chinese Porcelains Collected by Mr. and Mrs. Charles P. Taft,* New York, 1904, no. 24; *Catalogue of the Taft Museum,* Cincinnati, 1939 and 1958, nos. 235, 237.

1931.169, 1931.173

Rouleau Vase

Kangxi reign (Qing dynasty), ca. 1700
Porcelain, H. 43.2 cm (17 in.)
Mark: underglaze blue double ring

This famille verte rouleau vase is enameled in colors and gilt with shaped panels of scenes of romantic dalliance alternating with scenes of scholars in pavilions set in mountainous river landscapes. The shoulder is decorated with quatrefoil panels of chrysanthemums growing from pierced rockwork. All the enameling is on a deep powder blue ground with gilding and panels of flowering branches linked by flowering leafy scrolls. The ridged cylindrical neck is decorated with gilt sprays of orchid.

The four shaped panels, in reserve, of romantic encounters illustrate scenes from the fourteenth-century novel *Xi Xiang Ji,* or *The Romance of the Western Chamber,* or from one of the many dramas derived from this popular love story. The heroine, Cui Yingying, is depicted in a garden, seated on the lap of the young scholar-monk Zhang Junrui, while her maid, Hongniang,

1931.176

watches from behind rockwork. As Sheila Keppel wrote, Cui Yingying's yellow robe is decorated with *shou,* the character for immortality, which may indicate that she is the "Bridal *Du,*" who has risen from her grave to meet her returning lover in the *Mudan ting,* or "Peony Pavilion."[1]

The inclusion of the maid, Hongniang, whose name translates as "red girls," in the scene emphasizes her role as the intermediary between the lovers. In Chinese romances, Hongniang is a stock name for ladies' maids who typically assist in ensuring that love prevails.[2]

1. Sheila Keppel, *China in 1700: Kangxi Porcelains at the Taft Museum,* exh. cat., Cincinnati, 1988, p. 12. See 1931.164, p. 640, and 1931.184–85, p. 675, for other representations of scenes from *The Romance of the Western Chamber.*

2. Wolfram Eberhard, *A Dictionary of Chinese Symbols,* trans. G. L. Campbell, London, 1991, p. 238.

Provenance [Duveen, New York]; Taft collection, May 8, 1908.

Exhibitions Cincinnati, Taft Museum, *Ming to Ch'ing: Imperial Objects and Textiles, Masterpieces of Chinese Furniture,* Feb. 12–June 30, 1975; Cincinnati, Taft Museum [also Flint, Mich., and Muncie, Ind.], *China in 1700: Kangxi Porcelains at the Taft Museum,* Sept. 8, 1988–Sept. 17, 1989 (cat. by Sheila Keppel, no. 41).

Literature *Catalogue of the Taft Museum,* Cincinnati, 1939 and 1958, no. 240.

1931.176

1931.176 scholar in pavilion

Rouleau Vase

Kangxi reign (Qing dynasty), ca. 1700
Porcelain, H. 43.2 cm (17 in.)
Unmarked; incised collector's mark of a later date

This famille verte rouleau vase is enameled in colors with four large and six small rectangular panels of insects flying above flowering plants of chrysanthemum, peony, pinks, poppy, and

1931.174 detail of mark

1931.174

1931.170

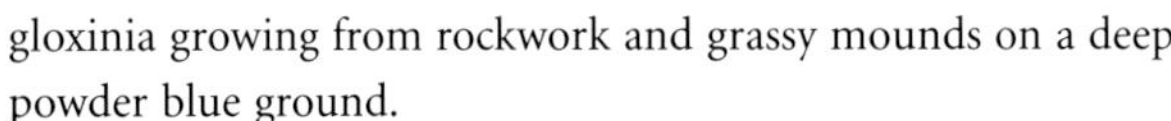

gloxinia growing from rockwork and grassy mounds on a deep powder blue ground.

Provenance [Duveen, New York]; Taft collection, Oct. 21, 1902.

Exhibition Cincinnati, Taft Museum, *Ming to Ch'ing: Imperial Objects and Textiles, Masterpieces of Chinese Furniture,* Feb. 12–June 30, 1975.

Literature John Getz, *A Catalogue of Chinese Porcelains Collected by Mr. and Mrs. Charles P. Taft,* New York, 1904, no. 25; *Catalogue of the Taft Museum,* Cincinnati, 1939 and 1958, no. 241.

1931.174

Bottle Vase

Kangxi reign (Qing dynasty), ca. 1700
Porcelain, H. 29.2 cm (11½ in.)
Unmarked

This famille verte slender pear-shaped bottle vase is enameled in colors and gilt with two quatrefoil oval panels of flowering chrysanthemum, pinks, and grasses growing from rockwork and with one panel of the *bogu,* or Hundred Antiques, all on an even powder blue ground with traces of original gilt bands of a key pattern on the neck and of branches between the panels.

Provenance [Duveen, New York]; Taft collection, Dec. 12, 1902.

Literature John Getz, *A Catalogue of Chinese Porcelains Collected by Mr.*

1931.170 the Hundred Antiques

and Mrs. Charles P. Taft, New York, 1904, no. 26; *Catalogue of the Taft Museum,* Cincinnati, 1939 and 1958, no. 46.

1931.170

Bottle

Kangxi reign (Qing dynasty), ca. 1700
Porcelain, H. 25.4 cm (10 in.)
Unmarked

This famille verte pear-shaped bottle has a slender trumpet neck with a convex ring below the lip and a slightly flaring foot ring. It is enameled with quatrefoil panels of flowering chrysanthemum with a butterfly and of camellia with a yellow bird and with small leaf-shaped panels of pinks and gloxinia, all on a powder blue ground.

Both the chrysanthemum, or *ju,* and the butterfly, or *die,* are symbolic of longevity. *Ju* sounds like *jiu,* meaning "long time,"[1] while *die* is a homophone for the word for seventy. The combination of the two motifs expresses the wish for long life continuing to age seventy.

1. Wolfram Eberhard, *A Dictionary of Chinese Symbols,* trans. G. L. Campbell, London, 1991, p. 63.

Provenance [Duveen, New York]; Taft collection, Nov. 21, 1903.

Literature John Getz, *A Catalogue of Chinese Porcelains Collected by Mr. and Mrs. Charles P. Taft,* New York, 1904, no. 27; *Catalogue of the Taft Museum,* Cincinnati, 1939 and 1958, no. 73.

1931.172

1931.172

1931.172 butterfly and chrysanthemum

Aubergine

Bowl

Early Kangxi reign (Qing dynasty), ca. 1662–75
Porcelain, H. 9.5 x DIAM. 19.4 cm (3¾ x 7⅝ in.)
Mark: unidentified underglaze blue two-character seal in double square within wide double ring

This deep circular bowl has the high cylindrical foot ring and everted lip typical of its date and method of production. It is enameled on the biscuit with scattered flowering branches on the inside and exotic butterflies among dense flower sprays and scattered leaves and prunus blossoms on the outside, all on an aubergine ground.

The combination of butterflies, or *die,* and prunus blossoms, or *mei hua,* symbolizes a wish for long life and immaculate beauty.[1]

This bowl is very similar in material and methods of enameling to those pieces known as *brinjal* bowls.

1. Wolfram Eberhard, *A Dictionary of Chinese Symbols,* trans. G. L. Campbell, London, 1991, p. 52.

Provenance Alfred Trapnell, London; [Duveen, New York]; Taft collection, Apr. 23, 1910.

Literature *Catalogue of the Taft Museum,* Cincinnati, 1939 and 1958, no. 226.

1931.77

1931.77

1931.77

1931.77 detail of mark

Famille Jaune

Shoulao, Daoist God of Longevity

Figure: Qing dynasty, nineteenth century; base: Kangxi reign (Qing dynasty), 1662–1722
Porcelain, H. 66 cm (26 in.)
Unmarked base with linen impression

This famille jaune figure of Shoulao, the Daoist god of longevity, modeled standing on a lotus flower, is set on a rectangular base decorated with dragons pursuing pearls within trellis borders. His yellow coat is enameled with cranes and peaches and decorated with gilt *shou* characters, all symbols of immortality; his

1931.177

1931.81 flowering lotus on exterior

1931.81 lingzhi spray in center

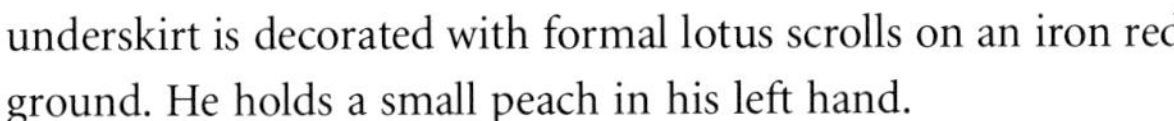

underskirt is decorated with formal lotus scrolls on an iron red ground. He holds a small peach in his left hand.

This figure of Shoulao was obtained by Duveen Brothers from Msgr. Alphonse Favier, the bishop of Beijing (then Peking); the Kangxi-period base on which the figure now rests was provided by the dealer. Both hands are later replacements.

Provenance Alphonse Favier, bishop of Beijing (in 1897); [Duveen, New York]; Taft collection, Apr. 19, 1906.

Literature Alphonse Favier, *Peking: Histoire et description,* Peking, 1897, pp. 27, 532, pl. XXXVI; *Catalogue of the Taft Museum,* Cincinnati, 1939 and 1958, no. 436 (ill.).

1931.177

Bowl

Kangxi reign (Qing dynasty), ca. 1662–75
Porcelain, H. 8.9 x DIAM. 23 cm (3½ x 8 in.)
Mark: underglaze blue *lingzhi* within double ring

This famille jaune deep circular bowl with high cylindrical foot ring and everted lip is enameled on the biscuit in aubergine, pale lime, and dark green on a clear pale yellow ground with lotus flowering in shallow water on the exterior and a *lingzhi* plant in the center of the interior.

The lotus (*Nelumbo nucifera*), or *hehua* in Chinese, is an important native plant in Chinese life, with each of its parts having a specific name and use. The leaves and roots, for example, are eaten, while the seeds are incorporated into medicines.[1] The tuliplike flowers of the lotus are cultivated for their ornamental beauty.

Imported from India along with Buddhism during the first century A.D., the lotus, which is sacred in Buddhist belief, is a symbol of purity and perfection.[2] Growing from mud but not defiled, the lotus is associated with Buddha, who was born into earthly existence but leads the way beyond to enlightenment. Because the plant is thought by the Chinese to bring rebirth, the life cycle of the lotus has come to symbolize the human life process.

The lotus is often represented in Chinese decorations as a symbol for marriage. For example, other names for the lotus in Chinese sound the same as *lian,* which means "to connect" and "to love," or *he,* "harmony."[3] A lotus flower depicted with a bud and a leaf represents a "complete union."

1. C. A. S. Williams, *Outlines of Chinese Symbolism and Art Motives,* New York, 1976, pp. 256–57.

2. Sheila Keppel, *China in 1700: Kangxi Porcelains at the Taft Museum,* exh. cat., Cincinnati, 1988, p. 16.

3. Keppel, p. 16.

Provenance Taft collection, after 1904.

Exhibition Cincinnati, Taft Museum [also Flint, Mich., and Muncie, Ind.], *China in 1700: Kangxi Porcelains at the Taft Museum,* Sept. 8, 1988–Sept. 17, 1989 (cat. by Sheila Keppel, no. 74).

Literature *Catalogue of the Taft Museum,* Cincinnati, 1939 and 1958, no. 464.

1931.81

Jar with Cover

Kangxi reign (Qing dynasty), ca. 1700
Porcelain, H. 26.7 cm (10½ in.)
Mark: underglaze blue double ring

This famille jaune oviform jar with domed cover is enameled on the biscuit in green on a pale yellow ground with a continuous loose formal flowering camellia-branch scroll. The shoulder and finial are decorated with iron red flowers and the base with an underglaze blue honeycomb.

The Chinese word for the camellia, *shan-cha,* is literally translated as "mountain tea" and also refers to an innocent young girl.[1]

1. Wolfram Eberhard, *A Dictionary of Chinese Symbols,* trans. G. L. Campbell, London, 1991, pp. 55–56.

Provenance [Duveen, New York]; Taft collection, Nov. 21, 1902.

Literature John Getz, *A Catalogue of Chinese Porcelains Collected by Mr. and Mrs. Charles P. Taft,* New York, 1904, no. 61; *Catalogue of the Taft Museum,* Cincinnati, 1939 and 1958, no. 287 (ill.).

1931.89

1931.89

Two Baluster Vases with Domed Covers

Kangxi reign (Qing dynasty), ca. 1700, with twentieth-century pottery replacement covers
Porcelain, H. (each) 15.2 cm (6 in.)
Unmarked

These two small famille jaune baluster vases with domed covers are enameled in colors on the biscuit with birds among flowering prunus trees growing from rockwork on thin pale yellow grounds.

Similar famille jaune baluster vases, but with period domed covers and described as early Kangxi, were formerly in the collection of H. J. Duveen.[1]

1. Edgar Gorer and J. F. Blacker, *Chinese Porcelains and Hard Stones,* vol. II, London, 1911, pl. 175.

Provenance [Parish-Watson, New York]; Taft collection, Oct. 30, 1924.

Literature *Catalogue of the Taft Museum,* Cincinnati, 1939 and 1958, nos. 290, 292.

1931.30, 1931.32

1931.30, 32

Pillow

Daoguang reign (Qing dynasty), 1821–50
Porcelain, L. 36.2 cm (14¼ in.)
Unmarked

This concave rectangular headrest is enameled on the biscuit in the famille jaune palette with long shaped panels of facing pho-

1931.163

1931.163 butterfly and archaic bronzes

enixes among formal peony scrolls. Smaller shaped panels of landscapes, a peach, a butterfly, and archaic bronzes in green, yellow, and aubergine are set on a cell-pattern ground. The recessed end panels are decorated with pomegranates surrounding peony branches.

The decorations on the recessed end panels of this pillow symbolize general wishes for wealth (peonies) and male offspring (pomegranates). A pillow with similar decorative motifs enameled in green, yellow, and aubergine was bequeathed to the Victoria and Albert Museum (London) by George Salting in 1910.[1]

1. See Edgar Gorer and J. F. Blacker, *Chinese Porcelains and Hard Stones,* vol. 1, London, 1911, fig. 42, and Rose Kerr, *Chinese Ceramics: Porcelains of the Qing Dynasty, 1644–1911,* London, 1986, p. 95, ill. 72, for comparison.

Provenance Taft collection, by 1904.

Exhibition Cincinnati, Taft Museum [also Flint, Mich., and Muncie, Ind.], *China in 1700: Kangxi Porcelains at the Taft Museum,* Sept. 8, 1988–Sept. 17, 1989 (cat. by Sheila Keppel, no. 77).

Literature John Getz, *A Catalogue of Chinese Porcelains Collected by Mr. and Mrs. Charles P. Taft,* New York, 1904, no. 57; *Catalogue of the Taft Museum,* Cincinnati, 1939 and 1958, no. 471.

1931.163

Square Tapering Vase

Qing dynasty, nineteenth century
Porcelain, H. 50.8 cm (20 in.)
Mark: underglaze blue six-character Chenghua reign mark (1465–87); not of the period

This square tapering vase with trumpet neck is enameled in the famille jaune palette on minutely crackled clear yellow grounds with panels of the flowers of the four seasons: spring, peony; summer, lotus; fall, chrysanthemum; and winter, prunus (see 1931.141, p. 672). The neck and shoulder are decorated with scattered flowering branches.

In the 1904 catalogue of the Tafts' Chinese porcelains, the vase is illustrated with hatched borders at the top and bottom of the neck, which have since been overpainted.[1] Although no specific mention of restoration of this vase is found in the museum's archives, it is likely that during the Tafts' lifetimes the neck was

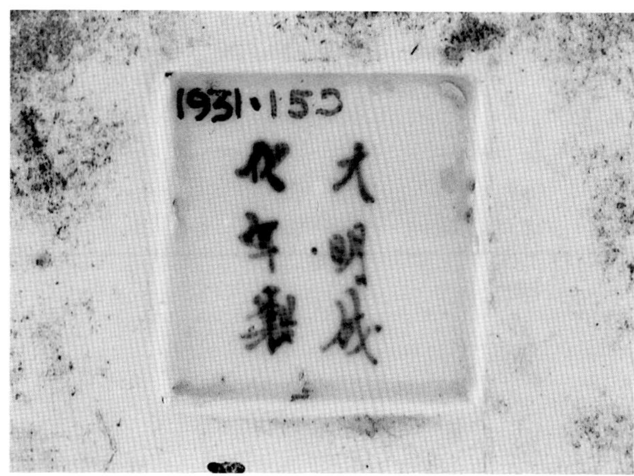

1931.153 detail of mark

1931.153

detached from the body of the vase and then repaired, with the current overpainting masking the damaged area.

1. John Getz, *A Catalogue of Chinese Porcelains Collected by Mr. and Mrs. Charles P. Taft,* New York, 1904, p. 98, no. 74.

Provenance Chang-Yen Huan, Chinese minister to Washington, D.C., and special imperial envoy to Great Britain at Queen Victoria's Jubilee; [Duveen, New York, with 1931.141 and a green-ground vase (now missing) as "set of three"]; Taft collection, Dec. 12, 1902.

Exhibition Cincinnati, Taft Museum [also Flint, Mich., and Muncie, Ind.], *China in 1700: Kangxi Porcelains at the Taft Museum,* Sept. 8, 1988–Sept. 17, 1989 (cat. by Sheila Keppel, no. 75).

Literature John Getz, *A Catalogue of Chinese Porcelains Collected by Mr. and Mrs. Charles P. Taft,* New York, 1904, no. 74; *Catalogue of the Taft Museum,* Cincinnati, 1939 and 1958, no. 437.

1931.153

Famille Noire

Beakers

Kangxi reign (Qing dynasty), ca. 1680–1700
Porcelain, H. 7 X DIAM. 8.6 cm (2¾ x 3⅜ in.)
Unmarked

This pair of famille noire hexagonal beakers is enameled in blue and aubergine. One is also enameled in yellow (1931.4). Both have flowering branches in petal-shaped panels on mottled brilliant black enamel grounds.

Provenance [Duveen, New York]; Taft collection, Mar. 1, 1904.

Literature John Getz, *A Catalogue of Chinese Porcelains Collected by Mr. and Mrs. Charles P. Taft,* New York, 1904, no. 56; *Catalogue of the Taft Museum,* Cincinnati, 1939 and 1958, nos. 301, 303.

1931.2, 1931.4

1931.2, 4

1931.4 detail of interior

1931.1

1931.5

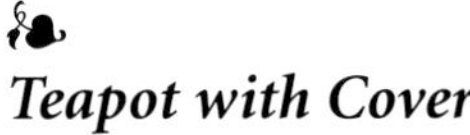

Teapot with Cover

Kangxi reign (Qing dynasty), ca. 1680–1700
Porcelain, H. 15.2 cm (6 in.)
Unmarked

This famille noire reticulated teapot with cover has a hexagonal baluster body modeled with a carp loop handle and a dragon-mouth spout. Each side is set with openwork panels of the *sanyou,* or Three Friends of Winter — the pine, prunus, and bamboo — above molded lotus petals and below a loose lotus scroll. The neck is decorated with *lingzhi* and brocades, and the cover with bamboo and prunus in openwork panels. The teapot and cover are enameled in colors and gilt on a thick black ground.

Provenance [Duveen, New York]; Taft collection, Dec. 12, 1902.

Literature John Getz, *A Catalogue of Chinese Porcelains Collected by Mr. and Mrs. Charles P. Taft,* New York, 1904, no. 50; *Catalogue of the Taft Museum,* Cincinnati, 1939 and 1958, no. 353.

1931.1

Teapot with Cover

Kangxi reign (Qing dynasty), ca. 1700
Porcelain, H. 16.5 cm (6½ in.)
Unmarked

This famille noire reticulated teapot with cover consists of a hexagonal baluster body modeled with a carp loop handle and a dragon-mouth spout. Each side is set with openwork panels of the *sanyou,* or Three Friends of Winter — the pine, prunus, and bamboo — above molded lotus petals and below a loose lotus scroll. The neck is decorated with *lingzhi* and brocades, and the cover with bamboo and prunus in openwork panels. The teapot and cover are enameled in colors and gilt on a thick black ground.

This teapot is slightly larger than the preceding example and is identically decorated except for the shoulder; this one has a tight lotus scroll reserved in colors and gilt on the black ground. The spouts on both teapots are shorter and tilted farther forward than on most other examples of this same reticulated shape.

A similar teapot, formerly at Burghley House (Stamford, Eng.),[1] was included in the Devonshire Schedule, an inventory of the contents of the house, made in 1688–90.

1. Sale, Christie's, London, July 13, 1959, no. 20.

Provenance [Duveen, New York]; Taft collection, Dec. 12, 1902.

Literature John Getz, *A Catalogue of Chinese Porcelains Collected by Mr. and Mrs. Charles P. Taft,* New York, 1904, no. 48; *Catalogue of the Taft Museum,* Cincinnati, 1939 and 1958, no. 355.

1931.5

Bowl

Kangxi reign (Qing dynasty), ca. 1700
Porcelain, H. 9.5 x DIAM. 19.3 cm (3¾ x 7⅝ in.)
Mark: underglaze blue lotus spray within double ring

This famille noire deep circular bowl with cylindrical foot ring is enameled in colors on the biscuit with flowering branches of magnolia, hydrangea, and peony growing among pierced rockwork on a black ground. The interior is decorated with scat-

1931.79

1931.79 detail of mark

1931.79 flowering hydrangea and magnolia branches

1931.79 detail of interior

tered flowering crab-apple branches on a faintly iridescent ivory white ground.

The combination of the herbaceous peony, also known as *fuguihua,* the "flower of wealth and rank," with the white magnolia (*Magnolia denudata*), or *yulan* (jade orchid), on the exterior of the bowl, and the flowering crab apple (*Malus spectabilis*), or *haitang,* on the interior, form a botanical rebus: *yutang fugui,* meaning "wealth and rank in the Jade Hall."[1] The Jade Hall is another name for the Hanlin *Yuan,* an official bureau established during the Ming dynasty with the purpose of compiling and publishing history treatises.

1. Sheila Keppel, *China in 1700: Kangxi Porcelains at the Taft Museum,* exh. cat., Cincinnati, 1988, p. 17.

Provenance [Duveen, New York]; Taft collection, Oct. 21, 1902.

Exhibition Cincinnati, Taft Museum [also Flint, Mich., and Muncie, Ind.], *China in 1700: Kangxi Porcelains at the Taft Museum,* Sept. 8, 1988–Sept. 17, 1989 (cat. by Sheila Keppel, no. 76).

Literature John Getz, *A Catalogue of Chinese Porcelains Collected by Mr. and Mrs. Charles P. Taft,* New York, 1904, no. 80; *Catalogue of the Taft Museum,* Cincinnati, 1939 and 1958, no. 460.

1931.79

Saucer Dish

Kangxi reign (Qing dynasty), ca. 1700, with later additions
Porcelain, DIAM. 17.5 cm (6⅞ in.)
Mark: four-character Chenghua reign mark (1465–87) reserved in white; not of the period

This small famille noire saucer dish is incised and enameled in colors; a roundel at the center of the interior depicts a green, yellow, and aubergine five-clawed *long,* or dragon, grasping a flaming pearl among clouds on a pale green ground. The well is

1931.90

1931.90 five-clawed dragon

1931.90 detail of mark

enameled in opalescent white characteristic of wares made during the Kangxi reign. The exterior is decorated with two dragons chasing pearls, incised and enameled against a "black" ground made of aubergine and green enamels.

Originally this saucer dish was an imperial ware with the simple incised interior decoration of a five-clawed dragon and the six-character reign mark of the Kangxi emperor, dating from about 1700, on the monochrome exterior. The false Chenghua mark — reserved against thick black enamel and surrounded by two *guilong*, clouds, and *lingzhi*, in green enamel — obscures the former Kangxi *nianhao* except for an underglaze blue double ring. The current color scheme and reign mark of the Chenghua emperor were probably added in China during the late nineteenth century to mask its imperial provenance before its export to the West.

Provenance [Duveen, New York]; Taft collection, Apr. 28, 1902.

Literature John Getz, *A Catalogue of Chinese Porcelains Collected by Mr. and Mrs. Charles P. Taft*, New York, 1904, no. 79; *Catalogue of the Taft Museum*, Cincinnati, 1939 and 1958, no. 364.

1931.90

1931.88

Dish

Kangxi reign (Qing dynasty), ca. 1720
Porcelain, H. 3.5 x DIAM. 20.8 cm (1⅜ x 8¼ in.)
Mark: imprecise underglaze blue two-character seal mark within double ring under clear glaze

This famille noire circular dish is enameled on the biscuit in the interior with panels of the flowers of the four seasons (peony, lotus, chrysanthemum, and prunus) in blue, pale aubergine, yellow, and green on a thick black ground. The black enamel ground was applied after the floral decorations but possibly also during the early eighteenth century. The exterior is painted with aubergine bamboo sprays under a thin opalescent golden glaze.

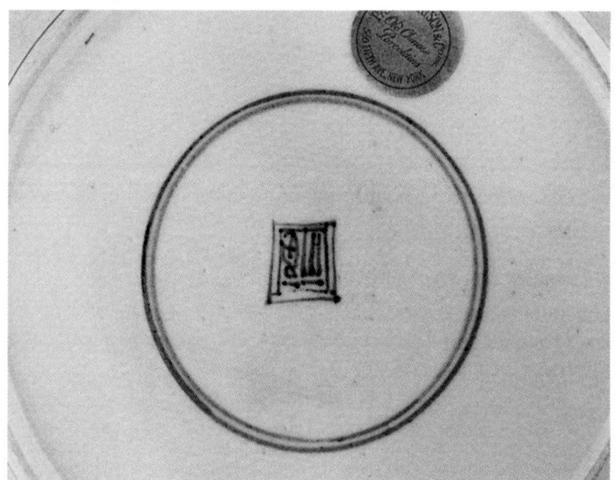

1931.88 reverse and mark

Provenance [Parish-Watson, New York]; Taft collection, Apr. 14, 1924.

Literature *Catalogue of the Taft Museum*, Cincinnati, 1939 and 1958, no. 428.

1931.88

Baluster Jar with Domed Cover

Kangxi reign (Qing dynasty), ca. 1700–1720
Porcelain, H. 62.2 cm (24½ in.)
Unmarked

This large famille noire baluster jar with domed cover is enameled in colors with faint traces of gilding reserved on a thin black ground with two long-tailed pheasants among flowering branches of magnolia, hydrangea, and tree peony growing from pierced rockwork. The neck is decorated with flowering branches above a yellow hatched collar. The cover terminates in a chrysanthemum-bud finial.

Provenance [Parish-Watson, New York]; Taft collection, Oct. 30, 1924.

Literature *Catalogue of the Taft Museum*, Cincinnati, 1939 and 1958, no. 476.

1931.147

1931.147

Oviform Vase

Kangxi reign (Qing dynasty), ca. 1700–1720
Porcelain, H. 18.4 cm (7¼ in.)
Mark: underglaze blue artemisia leaf within double ring

This famille noire oviform vase with a short trumpet neck is enameled in aubergine and green with a flowering white prunus branch reserved on a black ground. The short neck has been restored and was cut down approximately one-and-one-half inches.

Provenance James A. Garland, New York; [Duveen, New York, 1902]; J. Pierpont Morgan, New York (in 1904); [Duveen, New York]; Taft collection, Apr. 30, 1915.

Exhibition Cincinnati, Taft Museum [also Flint, Mich., and Muncie, Ind.], *China in 1700: Kangxi Porcelains at the Taft Museum*, Sept. 8, 1988–Sept. 17, 1989 (cat. by Sheila Keppel, no. 78).

Literature Robert Grier Cooke, *Catalogue of the Morgan Collection of Chinese Porcelains*, vol. 1, New York, 1904, p. 119, no. 778; *Catalogue of the Taft Museum*, Cincinnati, 1939 and 1958, no. 465.

1931.80

1931.80

1931.80 detail of mark

1931.78

Bottle Vase

Kangxi reign (Qing dynasty), ca. 1700–1720
Porcelain, H. 19.7 cm (7¾ in.)
Mark: small underglaze blue artemisia leaf

This famille noire bottle vase has a baluster body on a tall flaring foot below an elongated ribbed trumpet neck. It is enameled in yellow, aubergine, lime, and dark green with small birds among the flowering branches of a prunus tree growing from rocks reserved on a black ground. The foot is decorated with a band of green petals.

Provenance [Parish-Watson, New York]; Taft collection, Apr. 14, 1924.
Literature *Catalogue of the Taft Museum*, Cincinnati, 1939 and 1958, no. 463.

1931.78

Baluster Vase

Kangxi reign (Qing dynasty), ca. 1700–1720
Porcelain, H. 41.9 cm (16½ in.)
Unmarked

This famille noire baluster vase with trumpet neck and everted lip is enameled in pale lime, dark green, aubergine, and yellow with small birds among flowering branches of a prunus tree growing among low pine and narcissus leaves and blooms beside pierced rockwork, all reserved on a black ground.

The lip has been cut down. The vase would originally have had a tall trumpet neck.

Provenance George Salting, London; [Duveen, New York]; Taft collection, Oct. 21, 1902.

1931.156

Literature John Getz, *A Catalogue of Chinese Porcelains Collected by Mr. and Mrs. Charles P. Taft,* New York, 1904, no. 78; *Catalogue of the Taft Museum,* Cincinnati, 1939 and 1958, no. 132.

1931.156

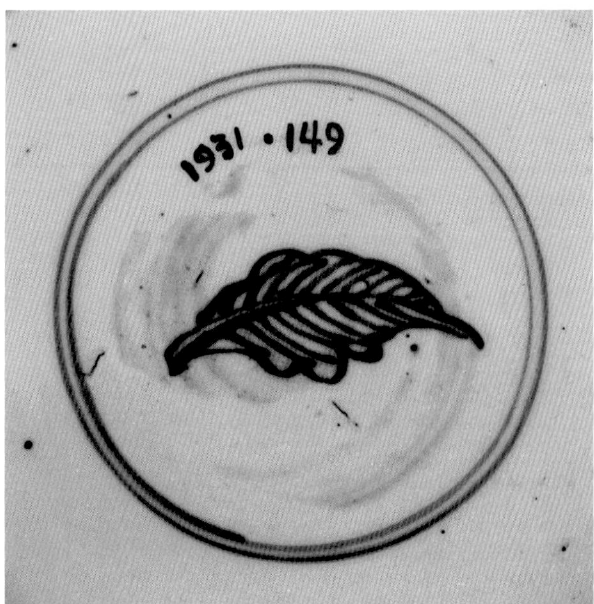

1931.149 detail of mark

Garniture of Baluster Vases with Domed Covers and Trumpet Beakers

Kangxi reign (Qing dynasty), ca. 1710–20
Porcelain, H. 39.5 to 40.6 cm (15½ to 16 in.)
Mark: underglaze blue artemisia leaf within double ring

This garniture of three famille noire baluster vases with domed covers and two trumpet beakers is enameled in famille verte colors, en suite, with shaped panels of exotic birds and flowering branches on thick black enamel grounds reserved with flowering chrysanthemum, tree peony, and prunus growing from stylized rockwork.

The cover to the central vase is a nineteenth-century French replacement by Edmé Samson. The flanking baluster jars have contemporary covers, probably from smaller vases.

Only two other similar complete garnitures of this type are known. One was formerly in the Morgan and Rockefeller collections. The other, formerly split between the collections of H.S.H. Prinz Johannes von und zu Liechtenstein and R. W. M. Walker, Great Britain, now forms part of the Wendy and Emery Reves Collection in the Dallas Museum of Art, Texas.[1]

1. The Reves famille noire garniture consists of three baluster vases with domed covers (one of which is a modern replacement) and two beakers, each marked with a period Kangxi underglaze blue artemisia leaf within double ring: inv. nos. 1985.R.957–61. Two of the covered baluster vases were formerly in the collection of the Prince of Liechtenstein (inv. no. 904), and in 1945 one baluster vase and two beakers were consigned by R. W. M. Walker (sale, Christie's, July 12, 1945, no. 97). The set was next sold by the late A. C. J. Wall at Christie's, London, Oct. 5, 1970, no. 149, and purchased by Wendy and Emery Reves. The Reves garniture was previously exhibited on loan at the Birmingham City Art Gallery, Eng.

Provenance J. Pierpont Morgan, New York; Mrs. Walter Hayes Burns, North Mymms Park, Hatfield, Eng. (by gift from her brother, J. Pierpont Morgan); [Parish-Watson, New York]; Taft collection, Mar. 1, 1926.

Literature *Catalogue of the Taft Museum,* Cincinnati, 1939 and 1958, nos. 315–19; David Torbet Johnson, "Taft Museum," *Ventura,* vol. IV, no. 16 (June–Aug. 1991), p. 141 (ill.).

1931.148–52

1931.148–52

1931.150, 148 replacement cover (left); period cover (right)

1931.150, 148 interior of replacement cover (left); interior of period cover (right)

1931.158

Baluster Vase with Trumpet Neck

Qing dynasty, late nineteenth century
Porcelain, H. 62.9 cm (24¾ in.)
Unmarked

This baluster vase with trumpet neck is enameled in the famille noire palette with flowering prunus growing beside rockwork reserved on a mottled iridescent black ground.

Provenance [Duveen, New York]; Taft collection, May 4, 1905.

Literature *Catalogue of the Taft Museum,* Cincinnati, 1939 and 1958, no. 474 (ill.).

1931.158

1931.141 prunus blossoms

Square Tapering Vase

Qing dynasty, nineteenth century
Porcelain, H. 51.1 cm (20⅛ in.)
Mark: underglaze blue six-character Chenghua reign mark (1465–87); not of the period

This square tapering vase is thickly enameled in the famille noire palette with the flowers of the four seasons (peony, lotus, chrysanthemum, and prunus) reserved on a black ground. The shoulder is decorated with flowering branches, and the neck is painted with birds among prunus. The unglazed foot in biscuit has a sunken glazed panel bearing the mark.

The neck is an eighteenth-century fragment replacing the broken neck of this nineteenth-century vase. Although the exterior of the neck is painted in oils to match the body of the vase, the interior is left undecorated, with the eighteenth-century porcelain clearly evident. This combination of two fragments — which were created about one hundred years apart — may be the result of a repair executed during the early twentieth century. Or, the eighteenth-century neck may have been used to suggest deceptively that the vase dated from the reign of the Kangxi emperor, thereby increasing its value at the time the Tafts purchased it.

1931.141 chrysanthemums

1931.141 detail of mark

Provenance Chang-Yen Huan, Chinese minister to Washington, D.C., and special envoy to Great Britain at Queen Victoria's Jubilee; [Duveen, New York, sold with 1931.153 (p. 663) and a green-ground vase (now missing) as "set of three"]; Taft collection, Dec. 12, 1902.

Literature John Getz, *A Catalogue of Chinese Porcelains Collected by Mr. and Mrs. Charles P. Taft,* New York, 1904, no. 76; *Catalogue of the Taft Museum,* Cincinnati, 1939 and 1958, no. 426.

1931.141

1931.154

Square Tapering Vase

Qing dynasty, late nineteenth century
Porcelain, H. 50.8 cm (20 in.)
Unmarked

This square tapering vase with a short trumpet neck is enameled in the famille noire palette with birds in flight among prunus branches in full bloom. The shoulder is decorated with flower heads, and the neck with butterflies and lotus, all on a creamy black ground.

Provenance [Duveen, New York]; Taft collection, June 14, 1902.

Literature John Getz, *A Catalogue of Chinese Porcelains Collected by Mr. and Mrs. Charles P. Taft,* New York, 1904, no. 77; *Catalogue of the Taft Museum,* Cincinnati, 1939 and 1958, no. 442.

1931.154

1945.1A–B

Famille Rose

The famille rose palette of enamels, introduced during the reign of the Yongzheng emperor (1723–35), differs from the earlier famille verte and its related variants, famille jaune and famille noire, in two important respects. First, famille verte overglaze enamels are translucent, while famille rose enamels are either opaque or semiopaque. The rose pink coloration, for which this palette was named, was new to Chinese enamels. Derived from colloidal gold, the low-fired rose pink allowed for the introduction of a much wider range of graduated tones, as in the Taft Museum's examples.

Suzanne Valenstein summarizes the other important difference:

> Second — and perhaps even more important — a lead arsenic, opaque white pigment was mixed with colors to achieve a range of color values for the first time. These new graduated tones allowed the artist to reproduce subtleties of shades and to model his drawing as the artist who paints with oils does. In addition, a variety of mixed tints was produced by combining colors, usually with the addition of the opaque white.[1]

In China, the famille rose palette is known by a variety of terms: *fencai,* or "pale colors"; *ruancai,* or "soft colors"; *yangcai,* or "foreign colors"; and *falangcai,* or "enamel colors." The term *yangcai* has led to the hypothesis that the famille rose palette may have been introduced to China by Jesuit missionaries who brought European painted enamels on metal substrates with them (see Philippe Verdier, "Limoges Enamels," pp. 328–30). Valenstein also writes that the palette may have originated with South German tin-glazed earthenwares brought by the Dutch.[2]

1. Suzanne G. Valenstein, *A Handbook of Chinese Ceramics,* New York, 1989, p. 244.

2. Valenstein, p. 244.

Beaker and Saucer

Yongzheng reign (Qing dynasty), 1723–35
Porcelain: beaker, H. 6.3 cm (2½ in.); saucer, DIAM. 13 cm (5⅛ in.)
Unmarked

This famille rose semieggshell beaker and saucer are enameled in colors and gilt with a woman standing on a terrace below a weeping willow. Her attendant holds her *qin,* a zitherlike stringed instrument, wrapped in yellow brocade. The borders are pink cell pattern reserved with floral panels.

The willow, or *liu,* is a symbol of spring and is also a metaphor for a beautiful young woman. The waist of a graceful, slender Chinese woman is often compared to the willow tree, and her eyebrows to willow leaves.[1]

1. Wolfram Eberhard, *A Dictionary of Chinese Symbols,* trans. G. L. Campbell, London, 1991, p. 314.

Provenance James A. Garland, New York (no. 436); gift of Louise Taft Semple, 1945.

Literature *Catalogue of the Taft Museum,* Cincinnati, 1958, no. 572.

1945.1A–B

Two Chargers

Yongzheng reign (Qing dynasty), ca. 1725–30
Porcelain, DIAM. 54 cm (21¼ in.)
Unmarked

These two famille rose chargers with shallow wells and wide sloping borders are enameled in colors and gilt. On one (1931.184), two fishermen are greeted by women and children on their return home, while an old man with a reed fan relaxes

1931.184

1931.185

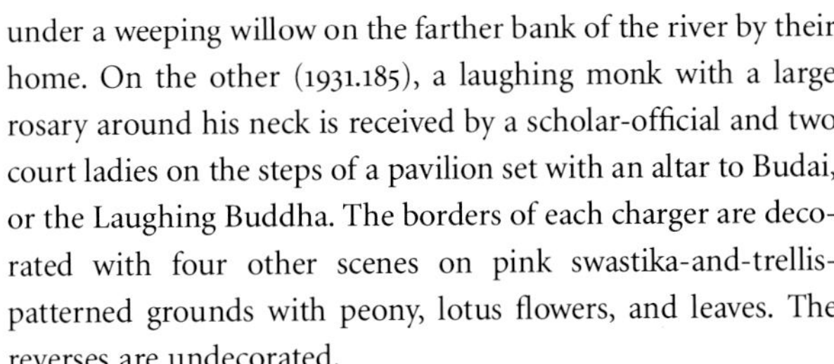

under a weeping willow on the farther bank of the river by their home. On the other (1931.185), a laughing monk with a large rosary around his neck is received by a scholar-official and two court ladies on the steps of a pavilion set with an altar to Budai, or the Laughing Buddha. The borders of each charger are decorated with four other scenes on pink swastika-and-trellis-patterned grounds with peony, lotus flowers, and leaves. The reverses are undecorated.

The scene on charger 1931.185 illustrates the episode "The Interruption of the Religious Service" from the novel *Xi Xiang Ji*, or *The Romance of the Western Chamber.* The subject is a version of the first meeting of the young lovers, the heroine Cui Yingying and the hero Zhang Junrui, a scholar studying for the national civil-service examinations. The scene on 1931.184 is not identifiable: the central female figure is costumed like Cui Yingying (as evident in the scenes on the borders of the chargers), but the story does not specify her meeting fishermen. This illustration may be an interpretation from one of the numerous dramas inspired by the novel.

Sheila Keppel has noted that "The Interruption of the Religious Service" was a factor in the decision of several emperors to ban the novel as a bad influence.[1] During the especially censorious period of the reign of the Qianlong emperor, the licentious aspects of the novel were publicly and privately condemned. In 1753 an official edict specifically forbade the translation of *Xi Xiang Ji* into Manchu. As Craig Clunas writes:

> [The scholar] Yu Zhi cites the cautionary tale of a youth of good family who wasted away in seven days after a surreptitious perusal of the dangerous text, while the later eighteenth century writer Wang Yingkui called it quite simply, "a book which advocates licentiousness." Numerous moralist literary critics consigned Wang Shifu [author of the novel] to hell for daring to write a work which celebrates so shamelessly the joys of sensual love.[2]

The four scenes on the borders of each charger, which are identical on both examples, also illustrate scenes from *Xi Xiang Ji.* At the top, Cui Yingying and Zhang Junrui are depicted during a clandestine meeting in the monastery garden at night. To the right are Zhang Junrui and his servant, probably waiting outside Cui Yingying's window. At the bottom Cui Yingying listens outside a window as her mother, Madame Zheng, interrogates the maid Hongniang. To the left Zhang Junrui gives a letter to a servant, probably announcing his success in the examinations to Cui Yingying.

1. Sheila Keppel, *China in 1700: Kangxi Porcelains at the Taft Museum,* exh. cat., Cincinnati, 1988, p. 12.

2. Craig Clunas, "The Western Chamber: A Literary Theme in Chinese Porcelain Decoration," *Transactions of the Oriental Ceramic Society,* vol. XLVI (1981–82), p. 78.

Provenance A. E. Cumberbatch, Eng. (in 1911); [Duveen, New York]; Taft collection, Apr. 1, 1920.

Exhibitions Manchester City Art Gallery, Eng., 1913 (according to Duveen invoice); Cincinnati, Taft Museum, *Ming to Ch'ing: Imperial Objects and Textiles, Masterpieces of Chinese Furniture,* Feb. 12–June 30, 1975; Cincinnati, Taft Museum [also Flint, Mich., and Muncie, Ind.], *China in 1700: Kangxi Porcelains at the Taft Museum,* Sept. 8, 1988–Sept. 17, 1989 (cat. by Sheila Keppel, nos. 42–43).

Literature Edgar Gorer and J. F. Blacker, *Chinese Porcelains and Hard Stones,* vol. II, London, 1911, pl. 221; *Catalogue of the Taft Museum,* Cincinnati, 1939 and 1958, nos. 469, 480.

1931.184–85

1931.97

Eggshell Deep Circular Plate

Yongzheng reign (Qing dynasty), ca. 1730
Porcelain, DIAM. 20.6 cm (8⅛ in.)
Unmarked

This famille rose eggshell deep circular plate is enameled in colors and gilt with a leaf-shaped central panel of a lady of the official class with two young boys before a scholar's table. The seven elaborate borders, which characterize this well-known type of famille rose plate, are decorated with flowers, dragon-headed foliage scrolls, chrysanthemums and gardenias, and a two-color gilt lotus-scroll band at the lip. The widest border has a pink cell pattern reserved with four pomegranate-shaped panels. The reverse is a deep monochrome soufflé pink.

This type of decoration, intended for the European market, is believed to have been enameled at Canton rather than Jingdezhen. After the eggshell wares were trimmed over a mold to the point of translucency at Jingdezhen, the fired but undecorated porcelains were sent by pass and river routes to Guangzhou, or Canton, where they were enameled in imitation of Jingdezhen designs but with additional borders to satisfy European taste.[1]

1. Sheila Keppel, *China in 1700: Kangxi Porcelains at the Taft Museum,* exh. cat., Cincinnati, 1988, pp. 8–9.

Provenance [Duveen, New York (as "very rare and highly valued by collectors")]; Taft collection, Apr. 28, 1902.

Exhibition Cincinnati, Taft Museum [also Flint, Mich., and Muncie, Ind.], *China in 1700: Kangxi Porcelains at the Taft Museum,* Sept. 8, 1988–Sept. 17, 1989 (cat. by Sheila Keppel, no. 30).

Literature John Getz, *A Catalogue of Chinese Porcelains Collected by Mr. and Mrs. Charles P. Taft,* New York, 1904, no. 46; *Catalogue of the Taft Museum,* Cincinnati, 1939 and 1958, no. 362.

1931.97

Saucer Dishes

Yongzheng reign (Qing dynasty), ca. 1730
Porcelain: 1931.114, DIAM. 20 cm (7⅞ in.); 1931.116, DIAM. 19.7 cm (7¾ in.)
Unmarked

Each of this pair of eggshell famille rose saucer dishes is enameled in colors and gilt with a lady of the official class and two boys playing among two large jars, a bowl of fruit, and a vase of flowers on a tall pedestal within foliage surrounds and cell patterns in gilt. One dish (1931.116) has a later copper rim.

The figural style on these plates illustrates the revival of the earlier, more naturalistic academy painting of the Song dynasty (960–1279) that gained favor from 1710 onward.[1]

1. Sheila Keppel, *China in 1700: Kangxi Porcelains at the Taft Museum,* exh. cat., Cincinnati, 1988, p. 9.

Provenance Comte de Vogüé (according to Seligmann invoice); [Seligmann, Paris]; Taft collection, Sept. 22, 1905.

Exhibitions Cincinnati, Taft Museum, *Ming to Ch'ing: Imperial Objects and Textiles, Masterpieces of Chinese Furniture,* Feb. 12–June 30, 1975 (1931.116); Cincinnati, Taft Museum [also Flint, Mich., and Muncie, Ind.], *China in 1700: Kangxi Porcelains at the Taft Museum,* Sept. 8, 1988–Sept. 17, 1989 (cat. by Sheila Keppel, no. 29 [1931.116]).

Literature *Catalogue of the Taft Museum,* Cincinnati, 1939 and 1958, nos. 341, 343.

1931.114, 1931.116

Ruby-Back Plates

Yongzheng reign (Qing dynasty), ca. 1730
Porcelain: 1931.95, DIAM. 21 cm (8¼ in.); 1931.99, diam. 20.6 cm (8⅛ in.)
Unmarked

These two famille rose eggshell circular deep plates are enameled in colors and gilt with three quail among flowering branches of chrysanthemum and camellia growing amid rocks. The wells and borders are decorated with panels of chrysanthemum, Buddha-hand citron, peony, pomegranate, and peach on pale pink cell-pattern grounds. The reverses are monochrome deep soufflé ruby.

Both the motif of the quail and the naturalistic, detailed rendering of the flowers on these plates derive directly from Northern Song dynasty (960–1127) court painting, such as the work of Li Anzhong (active 1119–31). During the reign of the Yongzheng emperor, renewed interest in modeling with light and shade was made possible by the opaque quality of the exquisite famille rose enamels.

The combination of chrysanthemum flowers, or *ju,* with quail, or *an,* creates a homophone for the phrase "autumn peace."[1] The panels of botanical motifs decorating the wells and borders of these plates represent basic Chinese wishes for lon-

1931.114, 116

1931.95, 99

gevity (chrysanthemum, peach), happiness (Buddha-hand citron), wealth (peony), and male offspring (pomegranate).

1. Sheila Keppel, *China in 1700: Kangxi Porcelains at the Taft Museum,* exh. cat., Cincinnati, 1988, pp. 16–17.

Provenance James A. Garland, New York (no. 691 [1931.95]); [Duveen, New York]; Taft collection, Mar. 28, 1908.

Exhibition Cincinnati, Taft Museum [also Flint, Mich., and Muncie, Ind.], *China in 1700: Kangxi Porcelains at the Taft Museum,* Sept. 8, 1988–Sept. 17, 1989 (cat. by Sheila Keppel, no. 79 [1931.95]).

Literature *Catalogue of the Taft Museum,* Cincinnati, 1939 and 1958, nos. 350, 352; David Torbet Johnson, "Taft Museum," *Ventura,* vol. IV, no. 16 (June–Aug. 1991), p. 141 (ill.).

1931.95, 1931.99

Baluster Jar

Yongzheng reign (Qing dynasty), ca. 1730
Porcelain, H. 89 cm (35 in.)
Unmarked

This large famille rose baluster vase is enameled in colors with scroll-shaped panels of elegant figures and children on palace terraces within deep ruby grounds reserved with white cranes and fruit and leaf-shaped panels of flowering branches.

The cover was made by the Edmé Samson establishment in the late nineteenth century to match the jar and has a seated Buddhistic lion finial.

A prunus tree flowering from a gnarled branch at the end of winter, as seen on the scroll-shaped panel of this vase, symbolized long life and was often incorporated into paintings given as birthday wishes for older men. Although completed nearly two decades after the Kangxi emperor's sixtieth birthday in 1713, the subject of this jar, with its idyllic domestic setting and long-life symbols such as cranes and prunus, suggests that the scene was based on one of the paintings made to celebrate the emperor's birthday, such as Leng Mei's *Garden of Perfect Celebration* (Cincinnati Art Museum, Ohio, inv. no. 1953.149).[1]

1. Sheila Keppel, *China in 1700: Kangxi Porcelains at the Taft Museum,* exh. cat., Cincinnati, 1988, p. 9.

Provenance [Duveen, New York]; Taft collection, Nov. 10, 1902.

Literature John Getz, *A Catalogue of Chinese Porcelains Collected by Mr. and Mrs. Charles P. Taft,* New York, 1904, no. 43; *Catalogue of the Taft Museum,* Cincinnati, 1939 and 1958, no. 6.

1931.183

1931.183

1931.178, 182

Pair of Baluster Vases with Domed Covers

Yongzheng reign (Qing dynasty), ca. 1730
Porcelain, H. 45.7 cm (18 in.)
Unmarked

This pair of famille rose baluster vases with domed covers is enameled in colors and gilt on soufflé ruby enamel grounds with double cash-shaped panels of cocks and birds among flowering rose branches; leaf-shaped panels of butterflies with sprays of peony, rose, orchid, and chrysanthemum; landscape scrolls; and fan-shaped panels on grounds scattered with chrysanthemum flowers. The necks are decorated with panels of flowers on lime green brocaded grounds.

The rooster, or *gongji,* is a lucky symbol in China often associated with the wish for success in the civil-service examinations, because the hat of a government official resembles a cockscomb.

The covers (1931.182 is a late-nineteenth-century French replacement by the Edmé Samson establishment) are enameled with quatrefoil floral panels and have chrysanthemum-bud finials.

Provenance G. R. Bevan, London; [Duveen, New York]; Taft collection, Nov. 1, 1923.

Exhibition Cincinnati, Taft Museum [also Flint, Mich., and Muncie, Ind.], *China in 1700: Kangxi Porcelains at the Taft Museum,* Sept. 8, 1988–Sept. 17, 1989 (cat. by Sheila Keppel, no. 28 [1931.178]).

Literature *Catalogue of the Taft Museum,* Cincinnati, 1939 and 1958, nos. 2–3.

1931.178, 1931.182

Baluster Vase with Domed Cover

Yongzheng reign (Qing dynasty), ca. 1730
Porcelain, H. 44.4 cm (17½ in.)
Unmarked

This famille rose baluster vase is enameled in colors on a soufflé ruby enamel ground with fan-, scroll-, and double cash-shaped

1931.180

panels of flowering poppy, hybrid vine, tree peony, Buddha-hand citron, and chrysanthemum. The ground is reserved with scattered chrysanthemum flowers between borders of panels of flower sprays on lime green brocaded grounds.

The cover with a lotus-bud finial is a late-nineteenth-century French replacement from the Edmé Samson establishment.

Provenance [Duveen, New York]; Taft collection, Dec. 12, 1902.

Exhibition Dayton Art Institute, Ohio, *Made in China: Chinese Export Ware,* Jan. 17–Mar. 1, 1987.

Literature John Getz, *A Catalogue of Chinese Porcelains Collected by Mr. and Mrs. Charles P. Taft,* New York, 1904, no. 42; *Catalogue of the Taft Museum,* Cincinnati, 1939 and 1958, no. 102.

1931.180

Hawk

Qianlong reign (Qing dynasty), ca. 1760
Porcelain, H. 37.5 cm (14¾ in.)
Unmarked

This famille rose model of a hawk is perched astride pierced rockwork with its head turned to its right. It is brightly enameled in colors and gilt with overlapping neck, wing, and long tail feathers on an iron red body and yellow legs. The rockwork is enameled in smudged turquoise, pink, and blue.

1931.179 side view

1931.179

As William Sargent notes, figures of hawks, especially in pairs, were popular with British and French collectors during the eighteenth century.[1] The Taft example was taken from the same mold as a pair in the Copeland Collection of the Peabody Museum (Salem, Mass.), for which Sargent lists possible eighteenth-century provenances.

1. William R. Sargent, *The Copeland Collection,* Salem, Mass., 1991, p. 150, pl. 68.

Provenance Comte de Vogüé (according to Seligmann invoice); [Seligmann, Paris]; Taft collection, Sept. 22, 1905.

Literature *Catalogue of the Taft Museum,* Cincinnati, 1939 and 1958, no. 333 (ill.).

1931.179

Pheasant

Qianlong reign (Qing dynasty), ca. 1760
Porcelain, H. 38 cm (15 in.)
Unmarked

This famille rose pheasant is modeled with its head turned to its left and perched astride a pierced outcrop of rock. It is enameled in colors and gilt with overlapping wing and long tail feathers on a pale iron red body. The rockwork is splashed with brown, pink, blue, and turquoise.

1931.181

1931.181 side view

Provenance Comte de Vogüé (according to Seligmann invoice); [Seligmann, Paris]; Taft collection, Sept. 22, 1905.

Literature *Catalogue of the Taft Museum,* Cincinnati, 1939 and 1958, no. 337.

1931.181

Oviform Vases with Domed Covers

Qianlong reign, (Qing dynasty), ca. 1775–95
Porcelain, H. 26.7 cm (10½ in.)
Mark: period enameled iron red four-character Qianlong reign mark (1736–95)

Both of these famille rose slender oviform vases with domed covers are enameled in colors and gilt on thick lemon yellow grounds. Each is decorated with a scene depicting two women carrying peonies in a vase and a basket; they walk with a boy carrying books near two white cranes among rocks and a flowering crab-apple tree. The covers are decorated with small gilt Buddhistic lion finials.

The Chinese refer to the peony as *mudan* or *fuguihua,* meaning "flower of wealth and rank,"[1] and it is often combined with the flowering crab apple, or *haitang,* as an auspicious symbol. In this case, the addition of white cranes, which are both a longevity symbol and a mandarin rank emblem, creates a rebus wishing for the small boy to succeed in the civil-service examinations and to gain an official post in the government.

1. Terese Tse Bartholomew, *The Hundred Flowers: Botanical Motifs in Chinese Art,* exh. cat., Asian Art Museum of San Francisco, 1985, n.p.

1931.109, 111

1931.109, 111

1931.109 detail of mark

Provenance J. Pierpont Morgan, New York (in 1904; each with a paper label: *F4/5*); [Duveen, New York]; Taft collection, Apr. 30, 1915.

Literature Robert Grier Cooke, *Catalogue of the Morgan Collection of Chinese Porcelains,* vol. I, New York, 1904, p. 12, nos. 4–5, pl. XLIII; *Catalogue of the Taft Museum,* Cincinnati, 1939 and 1958, nos. 424, 440.

1931.109, 1931.111

Pair of Jars with Domed Covers

Jiaqing reign (Qing dynasty), 1796–1820
Porcelain, H. 68.6 cm (27 in.)
Unmarked

Each of this pair of famille rose baluster jars with domed covers is enameled in colors and gilt with two quatrefoil panels of scenes from the Boys' Festival, a celebration of manhood for seven-year-old boys, held in China on March 5 of each year. The panels are on a dense millefleurs, or thousand flowers, ground made up of the following flowers: magnolia; morning glory; tree and bush peony; simple, double, and spider chrysanthemum; narcissus; lotus; Buddha-hand citron; pomegranate; hydrangea; gloxinia; pink; camellia; white and pink prunus; and hibiscus. The bud finials consist of peach, ripe pomegranate, and Buddha-hand citron.

The reserves on these jars depict wishes for success in examinations, a reference to China's unique centralized civil-service system. For more than two thousand years candidates seeking appointments as civil officials were selected nationwide by their scores in annual examinations. Since success in the examination would ensure prosperity and a change in status for the candidate's entire extended family, rebuses and pictorial entreaties were created as auspicious symbols that were believed to make the wishes come true.

Within the reserves on these vases are scenes of children at play. The banners held by two small boys in the foreground of the reserve depicting other children riding hobbyhorses read *zhuang yuan* and *ji di,* or "first place in the examinations." The millefleurs ground surrounding the reserves is a reference to the successful candidates in the national examinations, also known as the "flowers of the nation."[1] The Chinese refer to this type of ground as *jiacai,* or "mingled colors."

The bud finials on each domed cover depict the *sanduo,* or Three Plenties, forming a rebus expressing the wish for longevity (peach), make offspring (pomegranate), and blessings (Buddha-hand citron).

In the original invoice from Parish-Watson, New York (Feb. 17, 1928), the dealer states that "this pair of pots and covers came originally from the throne room of the emperor Ch'ien Lung's [Qianlong's] Palace at Peking." However, there is no mention of this provenance in the Bennett or Gorer and Blacker catalogues, and one would expect such pieces from the imperial palace to have been marked.

1. Sheila Keppel, *China in 1700: Kangxi Porcelains at the Taft Museum,* exh. cat., Cincinnati, 1988, p. 14.

Provenance Richard Bennett, Thornby Hall, Northampton, Eng.; [Edgar Gorer, London]; [Parish-Watson, New York]; Taft collection, Feb. 17, 1928.

Exhibitions Cincinnati, Taft Museum, *Ming to Ch'ing: Imperial Objects and Textiles, Masterpieces of Chinese Furniture,* Feb. 12–June 30, 1975; Cincinnati, Taft Museum [also Flint, Mich., and Muncie, Ind.], *China in 1700: Kangxi Porcelains at the Taft Museum,* Sept. 8, 1988–Sept. 17, 1989 (cat. by Sheila Keppel, no. 61 [1931.166]).

Literature *Catalogue of the Collection of Chinese Porcelains formed by Richard Bennett, Esq.,* London, n.d., no. 167, color ill. opp. p. 28; Edgar Gorer and J. F. Blacker, *Chinese Porcelains and Hard Stones,* vol. II, London, 1911, pl. 199; *Catalogue of the Taft Museum,* Cincinnati, 1939 and 1958, nos. 481, 506.

1931.166–67

1931.166, 167

Guanyin, Bodhisattva of Mercy

Jiaqing reign (Qing dynasty), 1796–1820
Porcelain, H. 83.8 cm (33 in.)
Unmarked base with linen impression

This famille rose figure represents Guanyin, the bodhisattva of mercy. She is depicted standing on a separate matched lotus base, holding an ambrosia vase, and wearing a flowered damask robe, bamboo-decorated cowl, and flowered long-sleeved white coat.

The manifestation of Guanyin on a lotus, offering rebirth into the Western Paradise, is related to the Amida cult, which was popular throughout Southeast Asia.[1]

1. Sheila Keppel, *China in 1700: Kangxi Porcelains at the Taft Museum,* exh. cat., Cincinnati, 1988, p. 11.

Provenance [Duveen, New York, as Yongzheng]; Taft collection, Apr. 23, 1910.

Exhibition Cincinnati, Taft Museum [also Flint, Mich., and Muncie, Ind.], *China in 1700: Kangxi Porcelains at the Taft Museum,* Sept. 8, 1988–Sept. 17, 1989 (cat. by Sheila Keppel, no. 34).

Literature *Bulletin of the Cincinnati Art Museum,* vol. v, no. 1 (Jan. 1934), p. 12 (ill.); *Cincinnati Fine Arts Journal,* vol. vii, no. 3 (Jan. 1935), p. 8 (ill.); *Catalogue of the Taft Museum,* Cincinnati, 1939 and 1958, no. 475 (ill.).

1931.168

1931.168

Chinese Decorative Arts

Descriptions: Anthony Derham
Commentary: David Torbet Johnson

Enamel

Basin

Qianlong reign (Qing dynasty), ca. 1740
Low-fired enamels on beaten copper, DIAM. 40.6 cm (16 in.)
Unmarked

This Canton enamel shallow circular basin with a flat foliate lip is painted in the center with a scene depicting an official on a terrace praying to a vision of Xi Wangmu, Queen Mother of the West, seated on her phoenix among attendants in clouds. The well is decorated with fruiting vine; the lip, with panels of fruiting and flowering branches of peach and peony, Buddha-hand citron and chrysanthemum, pomegranate and camellia, and quince and wild rose on yellow grounds with formal flowering branches and blue *guilong*, or serpentine dragon, roundels. The center of the reverse is decorated with a horned *guilong* roundel, stylized blue dragons, and green cracked-ice pattern.

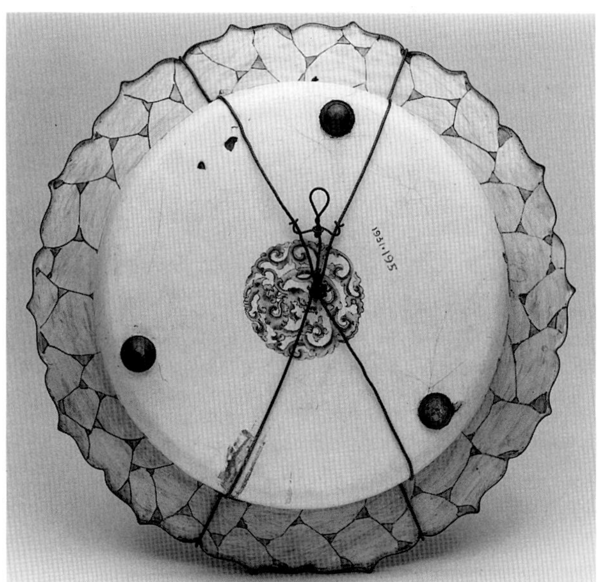

1931.195 reverse

1931.48

Cockerel

Jiaqing reign (Qing dynasty), ca. 1820
Porcelain, H. 23.2 cm (9⅛ in.)
Unmarked

This famille rose molded cockerel is perched on a pierced outcrop of rockwork. The lemon yellow body and legs are flecked with aubergine; the floppy wattle and comb are glazed pink; and the wing and tail feathers are carved in relief and glazed in black, green, blue, pink, and yellow. The rockwork is glazed aubergine over green to create a mottled, mossy brown effect.

A Chinese high official's hat resembles a cockscomb, and the word for each is *guan*. This cockerel visually expresses a wish for an official post or advancement in the Chinese civil service.

Provenance James A. Garland, New York; [Duveen, New York, 1902]; J. Pierpont Morgan, New York (in 1904); [Duveen, New York]; Taft collection, Apr. 30, 1915.

Literature Robert Grier Cooke, *Catalogue of the Morgan Collection of Chinese Porcelains,* vol. I, New York, 1904, case XXIII, no. 565; *Catalogue of the Taft Museum,* Cincinnati, 1939 and 1958, no. 356.

1931.48

1931.195

Literature *Catalogue of the Taft Museum*, Cincinnati, 1939 and 1958, no. 5.

1931.195

Jade

Vase with Cover

Qianlong reign (Qing dynasty), 1736–95
Jade, H. 24 cm (9½ in.)
Unmarked

This pale celadon jade vase with cover is carved as a plain oval vessel standing beside rockwork, from which grow the gnarled branches of a prunus, carved in high relief and openwork, on which perch two long-tailed birds.

Jade, or *yu*, symbolizes purity, and the skin of beautiful women is compared to its cool surface.[1] The long-tailed birds of this vase resemble magpies, known in China as *xiqiao*, or "joy bringing."[2]

1. Wolfram Eberhard, *A Dictionary of Chinese Symbols*, trans. G. L. Campbell, London, 1991, p. 153.

1931.374

2. Eberhard, p. 174.

Literature *Catalogue of the Taft Museum*, Cincinnati, 1939 and 1958, no. 569.

1931.374

Amber

Snuff Bottle

Qing dynasty, nineteenth century
Natural amber, H. 9.5 cm (3¾ in.)
Unmarked

This amber snuff bottle is carved in the form of Shoulao holding his staff and a peach of immortality and leading a maiden who is astride his stag. The maiden carries on her back a large bottle gourd, hollowed out to be used as a snuff bottle.

The Chinese term for amber is *hu-po*, or "tiger soul," and symbolizes courage. The spirit of a tiger, which the Chinese consider a courageous creature, was believed to enter the earth and become amber when the tiger died.[1]

1. Wolfram Eberhard, *A Dictionary of Chinese Symbols*, trans. G. L. Campbell, London, 1991, p. 17.

1931.375

1931.375

Rock Crystal

Shoulao

Qing dynasty, 1850–1907
Rock crystal, H. 15.2 cm (6 in.)
Unmarked

This standing rock-crystal figure depicts Shoulao holding over his head a fruiting peach branch, carved from a deep green colored inclusion, or foreign mineral, in the crystal. The base is fitted with a peg to attach the figure to a rockwork base.

Provenance [Duveen, New York]; Taft collection, Dec. 8, 1907.

Literature *Catalogue of the Taft Museum*, Cincinnati, 1939 and 1958, no. 12.

1931.198

Shoulao

Qing dynasty, 1850–1907
Rock crystal, H. 16.5 cm (6½ in.)
Unmarked

This rock-crystal carving depicts Shoulao holding a large peach of immortality in both hands.

Provenance [Duveen, New York]; Taft collection, Dec. 8, 1907.

Literature *Catalogue of the Taft Museum*, Cincinnati, 1939 and 1958, no. 14.

1931.200

1931.198

1931.201

1931.200

Shoulao

Qing dynasty, 1850–1907
Rock crystal, H. 22.2 cm (8¾ in.)
Unmarked

This rock-crystal carving depicts Shoulao holding a *ruyi* scepter. The figure is pegged into a cloud-scroll base.

Provenance [Duveen, New York]; Taft collection, Dec. 8, 1907.

Literature *Catalogue of the Taft Museum,* Cincinnati, 1939 and 1958, no. 15.

1931.201

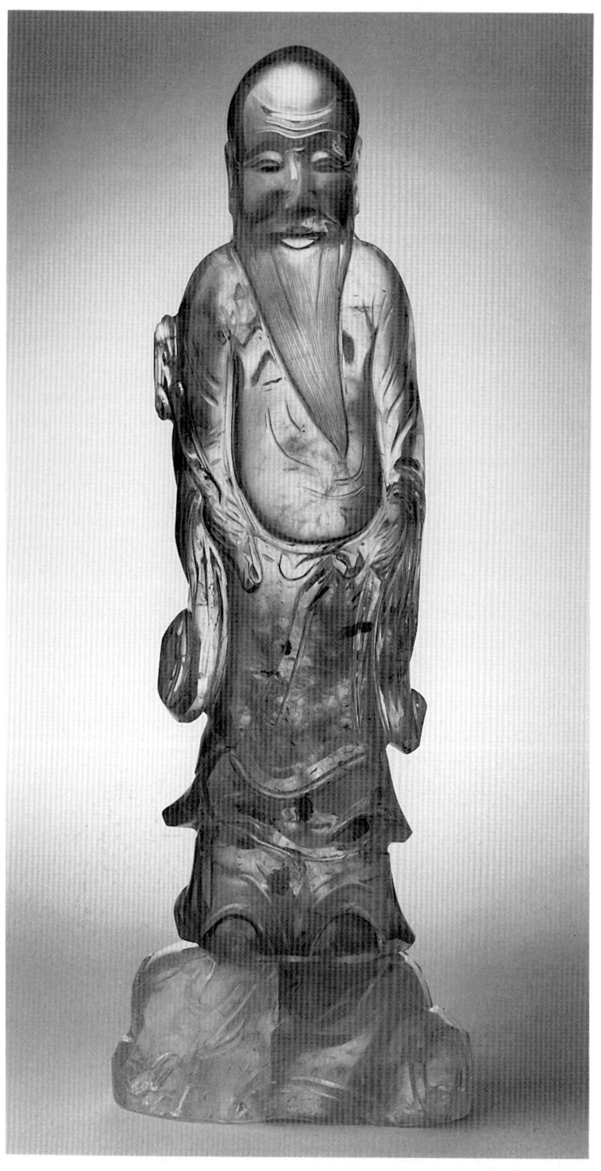

1931.202

Shoulao

Qing dynasty, 1850–1907
Rock crystal, H. 37.5 cm (14¾ in.)
Unmarked

This rock-crystal carving of Shoulao holding a *lingzhi ruyi* scepter is set into a rockwork base of cloudier crystal.

Provenance [Duveen, New York]; Taft collection, Dec. 8, 1907.

Exhibition Cincinnati, Taft Museum, *Ming to Ch'ing: Imperial Objects and Textiles, Masterpieces of Chinese Furniture,* Feb. 12–June 30, 1975.

Literature *Catalogue of the Taft Museum,* Cincinnati, 1939 and 1958, no. 16.

1931.202

Shoulao

Qing dynasty, 1850–1907
Rock crystal, H. 26.7 cm (10½ in.)
Unmarked

In this rock-crystal carving, Shoulao is shown holding the peach of immortality and his *ruyi* scepter.

Provenance [Duveen, New York]; Taft collection, Dec. 8, 1907.

Literature *Catalogue of the Taft Museum,* Cincinnati, 1939 and 1958, no. 17.

1931.203

1931.203

1931.204

Shoulao

Qing dynasty, 1850–1907
Rock crystal and amethyst quartz, H. 19.7 cm (7¾ in.)
Unmarked

This faintly smoky rock-crystal figure depicts Shoulao holding a fruiting peach branch over his shoulder. The figure stands on an amethyst-quartz cloud.

Provenance [Duveen, New York]; Taft collection, Dec. 8, 1907.

Literature *Catalogue of the Taft Museum,* Cincinnati, 1939 and 1958, no. 18.

1931.204

1931.205

Shoulao

Qing dynasty, 1850–1907
Amethyst quartz, H. 22.2 cm (8¾ in.)
Unmarked

This amethyst-quartz carving depicts Shoulao holding a large peach of immortality in both hands. The standing figure is adhered to an outcrop of rock.

Provenance [Duveen, New York]; Taft collection, Dec. 8, 1907.

Literature *Catalogue of the Taft Museum,* Cincinnati, 1939 and 1958, no. 19.

1931.205

1931.206

Shoulao

Qing dynasty, 1850–1907
Rock crystal, H. 20.3 cm (8 in.)
Unmarked

This smoky yellow rock-crystal carving depicts Shoulao holding the peach of immortality in his left hand and a now-missing staff, or *ruyi* scepter, in his right hand. The figure has been pegged into a rockwork base of whiter color.

Provenance [Duveen, New York]; Taft collection, Dec. 8, 1907.

Literature *Catalogue of the Taft Museum,* Cincinnati, 1939 and 1958, no. 20.

1931.206

1931.199

Immortal Maiden

Qing dynasty, 1850–1907
Rock crystal, H. 22.8 cm (9 in.)
Unmarked

This clear rock-crystal carving shows an Immortal maiden wearing softly folded long robes. The figure is now affixed to an outcrop of rock that was originally carved as a base for a more complex figural group.

Provenance [Duveen, New York]; Taft collection, Dec. 8, 1907.

Literature *Catalogue of the Taft Museum,* Cincinnati, 1939 and 1958, no. 13.

1931.199

1931.197

Boy Attendant

Qing dynasty, 1850–1907
Rock crystal, H. 15.9 cm (6¼ in.)
Unmarked

This rock-crystal carving depicts a boy attendant holding a lotus-leaf fan.

Provenance [Duveen, New York]; Taft collection, Dec. 8, 1907.

Literature *Catalogue of the Taft Museum,* Cincinnati, 1939 and 1958, no. 11.

1931.197

Glossary

David Torbet Johnson

an: A quail.

an baxian: The attributes of the Eight Daoist Immortals (or *baxian*), including the fan held by Zhongli Chuan, chief of the Immortals, with which he revives the dead; the bottle gourd and iron crutch associated with Li Tieguai, a lame beggar who uses his magical drugs to relieve suffering; the fish drum carried by Zhang Guolao, a recluse and magician of the Tang dynasty, who has the ability to foretell the future; the lotus, a symbol associated with He Xiangu as the patron of households; the flower basket, held by Lan Caihe, the patron of gardeners, who has the ability to make plants grow and blossom; the sword and fly whisk carried by Lu Dongbin, a sage warrior, who is the patron of barbers; the castanets, a symbol associated with Cao Guojiu in reference to his role as patron of actors; and the flute played by Han Xiangzi, patron of musicians.

anhua: A "secret" or "hidden" decoration either incised directly onto the body of the ceramic or applied in very fine slip. *Anhua* decorations can be difficult to discern because they are slightly obscured by the glaze but are visible when the object is held to the light.

artemisia leaf: One of the *babao,* or Eight Precious Things, often painted in underglaze blue within a double ring as a mark on the bases of ceramics from the Kangxi period. The artemisia (or mugwort, *Artemisia vulgaris)* is a fragrant plant associated with good omens and believed by the Chinese to prevent disease.

babao: The Eight Precious Things, which may include the ordinary symbols — dragon pearl, lozenge, stone chime, rhinoceros horn, coin, mirror, book, and artemisia leaf.

ba jixiang: The Eight Buddhist Symbols, which are auspicious signs, including the wheel of law, conch shell, umbrella, lotus, vase, two fish, and endless (or mystic) knot.

bay-lep: A yak-milk ewer or milk jug.

biscuit: A ceramic that has been fired without a coating of glaze. After this initial firing, it is decorated with either glazes or enamels and then fired again at a lower temperature.

blanc de chine: A European term for the white porcelain with fine-grained, vitreous body produced near Dehua, Fukien province, from the early seventeenth century onward. Made from local porcelain stone, blanc-de-chine wares are typically covered with a thick clear or white glaze.

bogu: The Hundred Antiques, or scholar's objects — a general collection of emblematic forms comprising the *babao,* or Eight Precious Things; the Four Treasures, or Invaluable Gems, of the literary apartment, including ink, paper, brush pen, and ink slab; the symbols of the four Liberal Accomplishments, including music, chess, calligraphy, and painting; and numerous conventional representations of sacrificial vessels, flowers, animals, and other small decorative motifs.

Boys' Festival: Celebrated in China each year on March 5, marking manhood for seven-year-old boys.

brinjal: A type of bowl about eight inches or less in diameter, either of conical or ogee form, roughly incised with flower and leaf sprays with yellow, green, and aubergine lead-silicate enamels applied directly to the biscuit.

cash: A decorative pattern derived from the square hole in the center of *Tamil Kašu,* a small coin or weight of money in China made from an alloy of copper and lead.

celadon: A high-fired green glaze that receives its color from small traces of iron and titanium oxides when fired in a reducing atmosphere. The term originated from Céladon, the shepherd in the stage version of Honoré d'Urfé's pastoral romance *L'Astrée,* who wore ribbons of a soft gray-green tone.

chimei: In Chinese, literally, "red eyebrows." The Red Eyebrows, a group of peasants and members of the Han nobility who painted their faces to resemble demons, led a series of uprisings during the period of the Three Kingdoms in an effort to restore the Han dynasty.

clair de lune: A subtle glaze, also known as *yuebai,* or "moon blue," of the palest cobalt oxide.

crackle or ***craquelure:*** A network of cracks in glazes resulting from the unequal contractions of ceramic and glaze, produced intentionally.

crazing: A network of cracks in glazes resulting from the unequal contractions of ceramic and glaze, produced unintentionally.

Dehua: A town in Fukien province near the locale where blanc-de-chine porcelains were produced at kiln complexes.

diaper: A rectangular or lozenge-shaped repetitive pattern.

doucai: Literally, "contrasted colors," but more often translated as "confronted" or "dovetailed colors." Developed during the reign of the Chenghua emperor (1465–87), the *doucai* technique combines underglaze blue outlines with overglaze enamel colors painted within them. After application of blue outlines under the glaze, the ceramic would be fired; then lead-fluxed colored enamels were applied on top, and the ceramic was refired in a muffle, or enameling, kiln at a lower temperature.

eggshell: A class of porcelain that has been potted to the so-called eggshell thinness.

enamel: Glass that has been colored with a metallic oxide. In the decoration of Chinese ceramics, enamels were painted on the surface of an underlying prefired glaze, painted directly on the surface of a prefired or biscuit body, or applied as a glaze on either an underlying glaze or a biscuit body. Since enamels fuse at low temperatures, they are fired in a special enameling kiln.

fahua: Raised enamel colors. A useful term, which has no real translation in modern Chinese, used to describe later Ming porcelain and pottery decorated with the cloisonné technique of applying thin clay threads to create raised outlines of the design.

famille rose: A term (along with famille noire, jaune, and verte) coined during the middle of the nineteenth century by the French ceramic collector Albert Jacquemart and used by ceramic historians and collectors as a quick-reference label to describe the predominant enamel color. The famille rose palette, introduced during the Yongzheng period around 1720, consists of opaque, very low-firing enamels with a lead-arsenate base. The predominant rose color is derived from a precipitate of gold chloride.

famille verte (also famille jaune and famille noire): The different families of enamel-decorated porcelains derived from the Ming dynasty *sancai* (three-color) and *wucai* (five-color) wares. Three-color wares were decorated in a combination of any three of the following colors: red, yellow, green, turquoise, and aubergine. Five-color wares included any of the above colors with the addition of underglaze cobalt blue. This Ming style carried over into the Qing dynasty when the earliest enameled wares were characterized by brilliant translucent greens (the famille verte palette, *yingcai,* or "brilliant colors") predominating over brick red, yellow, and aubergine with the addition from the mid-1680s of an enamel blue. From the low-firing famille verte palette of translucent, lead-silicate enamels developed famille jaune (with yellow predominating) and famille noire (with black predominating).

fenben: Sketches, such as wood-block illustrations, that are often sources for pictorial designs on Chinese ceramics.

fencai: Literally, "pale colors." A Chinese term for the famille rose palette. Other Chinese words for this palette include *yangcai,* or "foreign colors"; *ruancai,* or "soft colors"; and *falangcai,* or "enamel colors." The term *yangcai* strongly suggests that the technique of enameling porcelains in the famille rose palette was most likely known in Europe before China.

flowers of the four seasons: the prunus or plum, symbolic of winter and beauty; the peony, of spring and good health; the lotus, of summer and purity; and the chrysanthemum, of autumn and enduring friendship.

flux: A substance, such as lead, lime, or wood ash, combined with clay to encourage fusion during kiln firing, causing the body of the ceramic ware to vitrify.

formal: Pertaining to the use of conventionalized or stylized patterns of decorative motifs, particularly of floral forms in Chinese art.

foshou: The Buddha-hand citron (*Citrus medica* var. *sarcodactylis*), which is almost homophonous with the Chinese words for "blessings" and "longevity." The shape of the fruit of this plant resembles the fingers of Buddha; it is one of the *sanduo,* or Three Plenties.

Four Liberal Accomplishments: The four symbols of the scholar, consisting of music, chess, calligraphy, and painting.

fuguihua: Literally, "flower of wealth and rank," and also known as the "Prime Minister" of flowers. This Chinese term is one of many designating the herbaceous peony (*Paeonia lactiflora*). Another word for the herbaceous peony, which is one of the oldest known flowers of China, is *shaoyao.*

glaze: A glassy coating on the surface of a ceramic that both seals the clay body and decorates the object. Most glazes are composed mainly of silica and alumina, with other materials known as fluxes added to lower the melting point. Glazes may be applied to a raw body and then fired or applied to a prefired or biscuit body and then given a separate refiring.

gu: An archaic bronze beaker vessel.

guan: A cockscomb, which is a pun in Chinese for the hat of an official, associated with wishes for advancement in civil service.

Guandi: Daoist god of war. Historically a military hero, Guan Yu was a scholar during the Han dynasty, who, along with Liu Bei, a member of the royal family, and Zhang Fei, a former butcher, raised an army to reunite their country. A supporter of Liu Pei, the first emperor of the Han dynasty, Guan Yu was executed in A.D. 220. He was awarded the posthumous title of emperor or god in 1594 and after about 1600 became known as Guandi.

Guang-han gong: Literally, "The Palace of the Far-Reaching Cold," referring to the Moon Palace where Chang'e, the moon goddess, lives.

Guanyin: Buddhist goddess of mercy, originally the bodhisattva Avalokiteśvara, one of the princes who were contemporaries of the historical Buddha in India, who died in about 480 B.C. The bodhisattvas, especially Guanyin, lord of mercy, delayed their own enlightenment to help those on earth. Throughout the centuries the images of this Indian prince became increasingly feminine. By the eighteenth century, it was believed that Guanyin could appear in as many as five hundred different manifestations. A new manifestation of Guanyin as the maternal *Songzu* Guanyin, the Bringer of Sons, appeared after Jesuit priests arrived in China. In Chinese, Guanyin's name means "he who listens to the sounds (of the world)."

guilong: A serpentine dragon, usually depicted in profile with its mouth open, as found on Shang dynasty (ca. sixteenth–ca. eleventh centuries B.C.) bronzes. Among the first representations of dragons in early Chinese art, the *guilong,* like other dragons in China, is usually a benevolent creature. Nonetheless, unless the proper rituals are performed to appease these powerful forces, dragons might cause the lands to flood. The Great Emperor Yu (ca. 2205 B.C.), who is worshiped in the form of a salamander that somewhat resembles the *guilong,* is famous for reclaiming portions of China from such flooding by ordering that canals be dug to divert the water.

hai-mu: Mythical sea horses.

Hanlin *Yuan:* An official bureau established during the Ming dynasty to compile and publish history treatises. The Jade Hall is another name for the Hanlin *Yuan.*

haitang: The flowering crab apple (*Malus spectabilis*). The *haitang* is known in China as the "fairy" among flowers and is a favorite of Chinese artists.

hehua: The lotus (*Nelumbo nucifera*). This word is also a rebus for *lian,* or "to connect," as in marriage, and for *he,* a Chinese word homophonous with the word for harmony. The lotus is symbolically associated with summer, Buddhism, and purity.

hu: A tablet-shaped scepter held as an emblem of rank.

hu-po: Amber, which literally translates as "tiger soul."

huashi: Literally, "oily stone," a slippery stone used as a replacement for kaolin in the manufacture of Chinese soft-paste porcelain.

hulu: The bottle gourd, known as the calabash in the West (*Lagenaria siceraria*), which has numerous associations in China, including purity, longevity, and fecundity.

the Hundred Antiques: See *bogu.*

impressed rice-grain motif: A term coined to describe the kernel-shaped decorative patterns cut into the walls of ceramics and then coated with glaze. Rice was not actually pressed into the walls of the ceramic to produce the effect; rather a skilled artisan using a sharp flexible knife produced the motif. See also *linglong.*

jiacai: Literally, "mingled colors," a Chinese term for the millefleurs, or thousand flowers, style of decoration during the reigns of the Qianlong (1736–95) and Jiaqing (1796–1820) emperors.

jicui: Pale turquoise glaze first produced in the Qianlong period by adding arsenic to kingfisher blue glaze.

jinshi: A young scholar who has passed the imperial civil-service examination, thereby gaining a post as a civil official in the Chinese government.

juhua: Chrysanthemums (*Dendranthema spp.*). The chrysanthemum, a symbol of autumn, has been cultivated for centuries in China.

jun: A thick glaze used on stoneware from the Song dynasty originally produced at various kiln sites in Henan province, but subsequently made in Guangdong province.

kaolin: Literally, "high hills," a name derived from Gaoling, the locale outside Jingdezhen where this clay is found. Kaolin consists of alumina, silica, and water. The Chinese refer to this fine refractory clay as *tao gu,* or the "bones of porcelain."

Lange Lijsen: A Dutch term, coined by traders, translating as "long stupids" but later anglicized to "Long Elizas," for a style of decoration consisting of figures of slender, graceful Chinese women. In China these long-limbed figures are known as *meiren.*

langyao: Literally, "made in the kilns (*yao*) of Lang," a type of monochrome porcelain with shiny copper-oxide glaze, fired in a reducing atmosphere followed by a period in an oxidizing atmosphere.

Lantern Festival: A festival held on the fifteenth day of the first moon, at which time beautiful colored lanterns are displayed and firecrackers exploded.

lead glazes: A family of glazes in which lead oxide is the principal fluxing agent and which is fired at a relatively low temperature.

lime glazes: A family of glazes in which calcium oxide, or lime, is used as the principal fluxing agent and which is fired at high temperatures.

ling: The emblem of a commanding or imperial officer.

linglong: "Ingeniously and delicately wrought," referring to openwork or pierced decoration executed on unfired porcelain while it is in the leather-hard, or unfired air-dried, state. This technique results in extremely fragile ceramics and was often referred to as *guifu shengong,* or "supernatural workmanship," denoting a skill beyond normal human capabilities.

lingzhi: *Polyporus lucidus,* a dark, woody fungus that grows at the bases of trees in southern China. The *lingzhi* is highly prized by the Chinese as the fungus of immortality and serves as a wish-fulfilling or longevity symbol.

Luohan: Literally, "young man" but referring to a Buddhist ascetic monk, also known as Arhat. Traditionally in India there were sixteen Luohans, who served as disciples of Buddha, to which the Chinese added two more.

lung: A five-clawed dragon, associated with the Chinese emperor and his immediate family.

to lute: The process of joining two parts of a ceramic together using slip to seal the join, such as attaching spouts or handles to a vessel; also the slip used in the process.

mandarin: A European term for senior officials in the Chinese government. In Portuguese, *mandar* means "to command."

mandarin square: An insignia worn by officials in the Chinese government to display their rank.

mang: A four-clawed dragon.

meiping: A type of vase with a bulbous top and shoulders wider than its foot ring and a short narrow mouth, intended to hold a single branch of prunus blossoms.

mingqi: "Articles of the spirit," referring to tomb figures and wares produced to accompany the deceased into the afterlife.

mudan: The tree peony (*Paeonia suffruticosa*), the most popular botanical motif in China. Also known as the "King of Flowers," this flower is closely associated with royalty.

nianhao: The reign name assumed by Chinese emperors, which is also used as a means for dating Chinese porcelains. The name assigned to the emperor's reign has become associated in the West with the ruler as a person. For example, the emperor Xuanye is known in the West as Kangxi, the title he chose.

oxidizing atmosphere: During the oxidizing firing, the kiln is well supplied with oxygen, and the fire burns brightly.

pan zhang: The endless knot, or "long twist" in Chinese; see *ba jixiang*.

pastille burner: A vessel in which pastilles, or small fragrant tablets, are burned, producing a pleasing fragrance.

peach-bloom glaze: A monochrome glaze produced by spraying successive layers of glaze with different concentrates of copper, alumina, and fluxes. After reduction firing, the upper and lower layers of the glaze are clear; the middle layer is a colloidal suspension of minute copper particles. Larger particles of copper that reach the surface tend to oxidize to a green color.

petuntse: A component of porcelain, known in China as *baidunzi*, or "little white bricks." A felspathic rock known as pegmatite, petuntse is mixed with kaolin to produce porcelain and fuses when heated in a kiln. The Chinese refer to petuntse as *tao rou*, or the "flesh of the porcelain."

pingguoqing: "Apple green," the term for the classic glaze consisting of a high-fired bluish glaze under a translucent green enamel.

pipa: A stringed balloon-shaped guitar.

porcelain: A hard high-fired white translucent ceramic that resonates when struck. Porcelain is generally fired at a temperature in excess of 1,250 degrees Celsius.

powder: A type of glaze produced by blowing cobalt or copper coloring directly onto the raw body of the ceramic through a bamboo tube covered at one end with gauze. A clear glaze applied over the powder and fired results in a frothy, rich color, which can be further embellished with incised designs or gilding. Powder is known as "soufflé" when combined with the famille rose palette.

prunus (also *mei hua* or Japanese apricot): A genus of trees and shrubs including several domestic fruits such as the cherry, peach, plum, and apricot. In Asian art the representation of a Chinese and Japanese species *Prunus mume*, or the plum tree, is the symbol for winter since it blooms at the time of the lunar new year. However, the prunus is also considered the harbinger of spring. A popular motif in Chinese decorative arts, its name, *mei hua*, suggests beauty, or *mei*.

qilin: A mythical beast with the head of a dragon and the scales of a carp on the body and feet of a deer.

qin: A zither-shaped stringed instrument.

reducing atmosphere: During the reduction firing of ceramics, little oxygen is allowed into the kiln. Therefore, the kiln becomes filled with carbon monoxide that attempts to convert itself into carbon dioxide by extracting oxygen molecules from the iron or copper oxides of glazes. The process of extracting the oxygen from the glazes is known as reduction.

reserve: An unglazed area on a ceramic, protected from glazing by various techniques such as paper cutouts or wax, that is later decorated in enamels.

rockwork: A natural mass of rocks.

rouleau: A cylinder-shaped vase with short flat shoulders and a short thick neck.

ruby back or ruby ground: A name used to describe plates, saucers, and bowls of eggshell porcelain that are enameled in famille rose on the interior and in an opaque, deep ruby glaze on the exterior.

ruyi: A heart-shaped motif resembling the head of the curved fungus scepter, a ceremonial object carried by certain Buddhist deities and a symbol of monastic authority. The *ruyi* scepter is also associated with wish-fulfilling rebuses, since it means "as you wish."

sancai: "Three-color" glazes, although the colors are not necessarily limited to that number. Iron oxide in varying amounts is added to a clear glaze base to produce light yellows such as straw, amber, and brown. Copper oxide is used to create a range of greens, and cobalt oxide for blues.

sanduo: The Three Plenties, or the peach, pomegranate, and Buddha-hand citron, which form a rebus expressing the wish for abundance of longevity, male offspring, and blessings, respectively.

sanyou: Usually referred to as the "Three Friends of Winter," or the pine, bamboo, and prunus. These trees, which do not wither during the winter, are used metaphorically as friends who remain constant in the face of political adversity, the qualities of a gentleman, or the three religions of China (Buddhism, Daoism, and Confucianism). The pine (*song*) is a symbol of constancy in friendship, the prunus (*mei hua*) of good fortune, and the bamboo (*zhu*) of endurance.

shagreen: Untanned leather with a rough granular surface, prepared from the skin of sharks and frequently dyed green.

shan-cha: The camellia flower, literally meaning "mountain tea" but also referring to an innocent young girl.

sheng: A reed pipe; homophonous with "birth" and often found in rebus designs.

shou: The Chinese character for immortality.

slip: A mixture of clay and water used as coating or binding material.

soft-paste porcelain: A somewhat inaccurate term used to describe a type of porcelain made from a clay incorporating *huashi*, or "slippery stone" (talc or soapstone, also known as steatite), as a replacement for kaolin in the manufacture. Soft-paste porcelain is a particularly receptive surface for underglaze cobalt blue painting.

soufflé: *See* powder.

stoneware: Vitrified, high-fired ceramics made of clay and fired in excess of 1,200 degrees Celsius. Unlike porcelain, it may be either light or dark in color and is not translucent. The Chinese do not distinguish between fine stoneware and porcelain.

taotie: A highly stylized face or top jaw of a dragon intended to ward off evil, used extensively as a decorative motif on archaic bronzes and repopularized during the eighteenth-century Chinese fashion for archaism.

Three Star Gods of Daoism: Shoulao, god of longevity, often seen holding a staff or a peach of immortality and mounted on a stag, represented by the character *shou,* or longevity; also known as Shou Xing. Fu Xing, the god of blessings, who often carries a young child, represented by the character *fu,* or happiness. Lu Xing, the god of rank and emolument, who is attired in court robes, represented by the character *lu,* or rank. Together, these three gods protect all households in China and are believed to make the Chinese peoples' wishes come true.

touhu: An archaic Chinese bronze vessel with pierced handles, or ears, associated with the game of pitchpot.

wan: Ten thousand.

wang: A character that serves as an emblem of royal power.

wujin: A "black bronze" glaze, a combination of iron and manganese oxides with traces of cobalt and copper, resulting in a thick black mirrorlike surface.

Xi Wangmu: The Queen Mother of the West, traditionally shown with her eight horses or riding on her phoenix, is a legendary being who dwells in the legendary Kunlan Mountains in a large and beautiful palace surrounded by grounds where the peaches of immortality grow.

yangcai: Literally, "foreign colors"; see *fencai.*

yingcai: Literally, "brilliant colors," a Chinese term for the famille verte palette of decorating Chinese ceramics.

yin yang: A Daoist symbol that represents the duality of the universe, encompassing such principles as negative and positive, heaven and earth, and male and female.

yu: Jade, symbolizing purity.

yuebai: See clair de lune.

yulan: Literally, "jade orchid," a Chinese term for the white magnolia (*Magnolia denudata).*

zaju: A type of Chinese drama that incorporates singing and acrobatics.

Traditional Shapes in Chinese Porcelain

1 Early jar
2 *Meiping*
3 Pear-shaped bottle
4 Wine jar
5 Vase with ring handles
6 Archaic handled vase
7 Ewer of Persian form
8 'Monk's cap' ewer
9 Double gourd vase
10 Leys vase
11 Bulbous lipped vase
12 Square baluster vase
13 Pilgrim flask or bottle
14 Incense burner *(Ting)*
15 *Yen yen* vase
16 Rouleau vase
17 Bottle with slender neck
18 Conical bowl
19 Stem cup
20 Saucer dish
21 Plain bowl
22 Plain bowl with everted lip
23 Bowl with lion mask handles

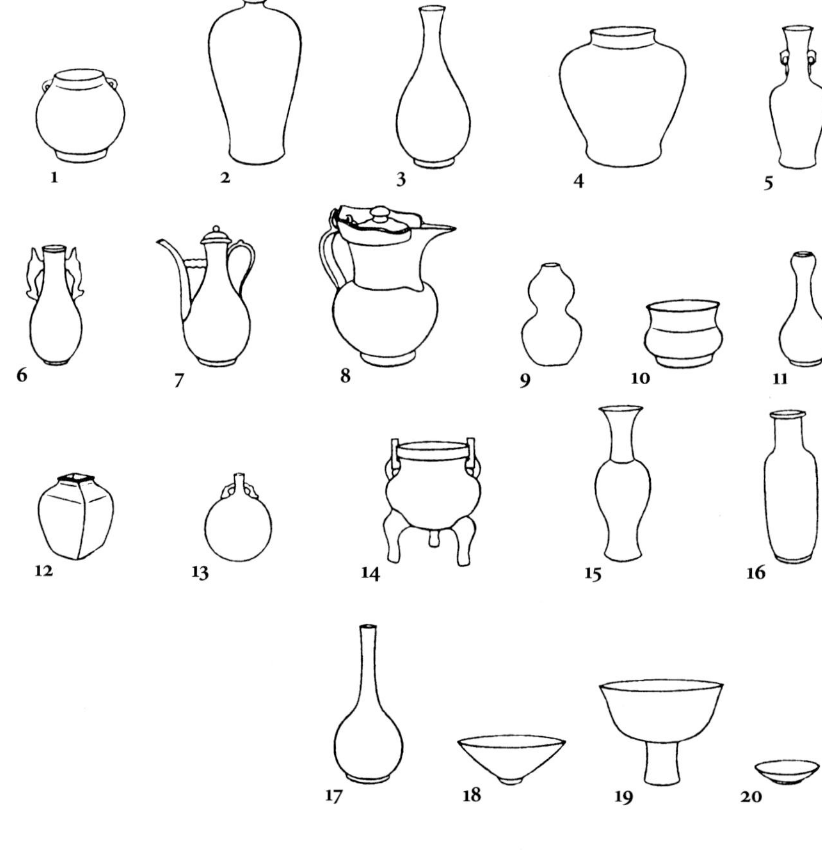

Index of Accession Numbers

Index

Page numbers in *italics* refer to illustrations.